STAND OU

GET NOTICED

BE BRILLIANT

SHINE

COMMUNICATE YOUR WAY TO A **BRIGHTER CAREER**

GERRY LEWIS

Praise for

SHINE

"Gerry's fresh and extremely practical insights will, without question, provide countless people with the right tools and a path to become much more successful in their careers. I took so many terrific things away from this book. I couldn't stop writing notes while reading it, and I can't wait to share this book with my employees and watch them learn and 'shine'!"

— Kathy Gregory, President & CEO, Paradigm Quest Inc.

"Gerry brings to bear in *SHINE* his amazing communication skills, which I have personally seen and admired. When we realize how much of our time is actually spent leading meetings, doing presentations and communicating with our teams, stakeholders and media to get the results we want, we realize that getting the communication right should be the biggest priority. Few of us are natural communicators like Gerry but the good news is that each one of us can become a good communicator. To achieve this, Gerry's book is a must. The presentation of the book itself is inviting. This is a book you will always keep with you and refer back to."

— Usha Thorat, Former Deputy Governor, Reserve Bank of India

"A helpful guide for young executives looking to improve their communication and presentation skills."

— Jonathan Weisz, Partner, Torys LLP

"*SHINE: Stand Out, Get Noticed, Be Brilliant,* Gerry Lewis' communication primer, is the new bible for best practices in all types of corporate and personal interactions. Whether you are presenting, informing, listening, influencing or managing change, Lewis turns his years of experience into practical tips and techniques on how to shine, command attention and be your personal best."

— Heather Campbell, Former CIO, Canadian Pacific Railway

"I've had the pleasure of working with Gerry Lewis on many occasions over the past 10 years, and have always appreciated and admired his ability to fully engage and energize his audience. His passion and commitment, and his exceptional facilitation and communication skills have absolutely been the key to turning our conferences from good to brilliant! It's wonderful that Gerry is sharing his insights and expertise through *SHINE*, a very practical, straightforward and entertaining resource for improving communication effectiveness."

— Wendy Hannam, Executive Vice President, Latin America, Scotiabank

"The pursuit of excellence is a continuous and mindful process. Gerry's insights and advice are practical, humorous and thought-provoking. This book is a must-read for college or university students before they hit the workforce, to ensure they can shine at communicating – an essential skill."

— Dr. Catherine Chandler-Crichlow, Executive Director, Centre of Excellence in Financial Services Education (CoE)

"In *SHINE*, Gerry Lewis, one of the most effective, engaging and dynamic communicators I have ever met, shares some of the secrets and techniques that underpin his dazzle. As life is entirely an exercise in connecting with the outside world and communicating, everyone should find in this book some ideas for improving their skills, whether it is how to achieve successful outcomes from meetings and teleconferences, keeping an audience in thrall, illuminating complex issues, or effecting attitude adjustments essential to change management at work and in life. I have made my own list, which I intend to implement post haste."

— Andrea Corcoran, Founding Principal of Align International,
LLC, a bespoke regulatory consulting firm

"This book is a wonderful, easy-to-read and, more importantly, easy-to-apply guide. I had a good chuckle in several places as I recalled times I have sat in unproductive meetings, been disengaged during a presentation, been totally frustrated with a speaker and felt irritated beyond words. I would encourage people to read this book and truly absorb the advice given. Some of us may take our natural communication strengths for granted, but many people in the working world fail bitterly at basic communication."

— Beverly Furman, Head of Supervision. Strate,
South Africa's Central Securities Depository (CSD)

"Throughout this deeply engaging book, Gerry radiates positivity, enthusiasm and excellence. The case studies provide practical, and often personal, examples of lessons learned. Gerry and his book 'shine' in every sense of the word!"

— Ilana Singer, Vice-President, Canadian Investor Protection Fund

"*SHINE* offers great advice, in a very practical and accessible way. The structure of the book – main text, recap, questions, action steps and notes – helps the reader digest the material and will encourage them to revisit the book after the first reading."

— Jan Willem van der Vossen, Former Advisor in the Monetary and Capital Markets Department of the IMF

"Gerry Lewis is a great communicator. Now I know why. Read this book, then try out some of Gerry's very practical tips. I wish I had read this book 30 years ago."

— Clive Briault, Senior Advisor, KPMG

"I have observed, learned and lived the key principles outlined in *SHINE*. They are real, and they work."

— Chris Hodgson, Group Head, Global Wealth & Insurance, Scotiabank

"This is a book about the talent and abilities you already possess, how to acknowledge them and what steps are required to bring them to the fore and 'shine'. Gerry Lewis covers the most likely obstacles encountered when communicating, as well as the use of body language to put people at ease, and ways to understand what they feel as well as what they think. All manner of useful tips, games and stories are part of Gerry's kit to help you succeed. Easy to read and easy to remember, Gerry's book will help you 'shine' because it shines!"

— Rosario Patron, Former Head of Financial Regulation of the Superintendence of Financial Services of the Central Bank of Uruguay

"*SHINE* can help professionals achieve excellence in their careers by using the various communication skills outlined by Gerry."

— Anatol von Hahn, Group Head, Canadian Banking, Scotiabank

Published by Think Up Communications Inc.
90 Trinity Street, Suite 503, Toronto, Ontario M5A 0E4

Library and Archives Canada Cataloguing in Publication

Lewis, Gerry, 1964-, author
        Shine : stand out, get noticed, be brilliant : communicate
your way to a brighter career / Gerry Lewis.

Includes index.
ISBN 978-0-9938766-0-8 (pbk.)

        1. Business communication. I. Title.

HF5718.L46 2014   651.7
C2014-906304-0

Developed and produced by the Dream Team:

Project Management: Amanda Persaud
Developmental and Copy Editing: Donna Papacosta
Copy Editing: Kevin Makra
Interior Design and Layout: Jeff Tappenden
Proofreading and Indexing: Martha Muzychka
Proofreading: Sue Horner

Cover Design: Kevin Cockburn/PageWave Graphics Inc.

Printed in Canada

Foreword

How many of us grew up singing the song about "this little light of mine" that we were going to let it shine? Not only were we going to let it shine, we were also going to prevent it from being blown out, hidden under a bush or taken around the block. Bottom line, it was going to shine!

Somewhere between the enthusiasm of a childhood song and real life, many of us seem to have forgotten our individual ability to shine. In this book, Gerry Lewis reminds us it is within each of us to truly shine – to be noticed and remembered – as an effective communicator, as a team member and as a leader.

Working with Gerry on many occasions over the years – in fact, decades – I have learned first-hand the passion he brings to his own communications, presentations and connections, as well as his desire to include everyone in this journey and to help them to find their own way to shine.

This book takes the same approach, seeking to engage the reader, providing many relatable experiences and ample opportunity for reflection. Gerry challenges the reader to try new approaches.

In my experience, I have found that communication is at the core of the success of a strategy, project or team, for people's ideas to be expressed, listened to and most importantly, heard and embraced.

Not only is communication one of the biggest factors of success, it is one of the hardest to get right. But like the childhood song says, you should not let anything get in the way of your time to shine.

As Gerry points out, your strongest ally – and opponent – to success is you. Being your own ally when it comes to communicating and presenting takes understanding, preparation and practice, ultimately enabling you to build the confidence you need to avoid self-doubt and be ready to take the stage when it counts.

SHINE takes an engaging approach to teaching ways to enhance your participation in meetings, to make compelling presentations, to lead change in an ever-evolving workplace and to really connect with others and grow your network.

Communication is a journey throughout your career, and in life. Throughout the book, Gerry helps you "hear" the communication from the listeners' perspective, walks you through the common pitfalls and challenges, and provides you with a framework to develop a plan for intentional and effective communication. The question-and-answer section at the end of each chapter keeps the discussion interactive and meaningful.

This book is not about using a formula or suggesting the best way to communicate. It is about all of us finding our own way to stand out and make an impact in our authentic and genuine voice.

Whether you are just starting out or are a practiced communicator, this book has something to offer. Perhaps its most important message is that we all have the right to shine and a responsibility to not let that be extinguished.

Enjoy the journey!

Arlene Russell
Scotiabank

To my Mom and Dad:
Thank you for instilling in me from a very young age that everything
I need to be successful is already inside me.

To Gaetano, my North Star:
Thank you for convincing me that a blank screen can turn into a book.

To my Dream Team:
Every edit, idea and comment breathed life into this book. Thank you!

Table of Contents

*"Why fit in when you were born to **stand out?**"*

— Dr. Seuss, American writer, poet and cartoonist

Introduction:

Stand out. Get noticed.
Be brilliant.

In work, as in life, we want to make a positive impact and a difference, and we want to be recognized for what we contribute. But when everyone in the organization is working towards this goal, it's difficult to stand out from the rest.

I have learned that the best way to differentiate yourself from others is through excellence. And what I love about excellence is that the harder you work at it, the more it pays off. Excellence comes when we are able to round out, fine-tune and polish what we already do well. Excellence is never given and can only be earned.

This book is about my journey of rounding out, fine-tuning and polishing my communication skills. Excellence is absolutely achievable and well worth the effort. Just ask Amanda.

Amanda's Story

STEVE:
What else do we need to cover for today?

ALICE:
We need to go through the candidates for Mary's replacement.

STEVE:
Oh yes, I reviewed the three candidates last night; what do you think, Karim?

KARIM:
They're all good fits to replace Mary. All of them have the background and experience that make any one of them a good candidate.

ALICE:
I agree, but remember we talked about expanding Mary's role to take on more of a project lead in the upcoming year.

STEVE:
Yes, good point, Alice. The role will head up bringing together our three divisions. There'll be lots of change in the coming year.

KARIM:
Well in that case I would go for Jeff. He has a solid background here and he did some good work for us on our last acquisition.

ALICE:
Yes, he did, but I think we're looking for someone who can also lead people through change. Didn't Amanda present last month on one of your initiatives, Steve? She really impressed me on how she was able to create the story of change.

STEVE:
She did. And you're right, Alice. She not only did a great job on the presentation, but I have also seen her confidence grow in the last few months. She has a way of getting the message across to people – that's what we need in this role.

KARIM:
I like Jeff, but I do agree with you both. Amanda stands out for me when I look at the three candidates, given what we're looking for.

STEVE:
Good, we've selected.

ALICE:
I'll let her know this afternoon. This will make her weekend.

In the scenario above, Amanda stood out for Karim, Steve and Alice even though all the candidates were qualified and ready for the promotion. Why did she stand out? Because Amanda was able to present herself in a way that got her noticed, and more importantly, remembered. Amanda was able to shine.

They say at some point, everyone will get their "15 minutes of fame." That may or may not be true, but I know with great certainty that each of us will get the opportunity to shine as a communicator – as often as we like.

Why "shine"? Shining for me represents a number of things. From an observer's perspective, when you shine, you stand out, you are noticed and you emit a brightness and a positivity in the situation or event. From your own perspective, when you shine, you feel warm, comfortable and "in the zone." When you shine, you feel confident, strong and happy.

Shining as a communicator does not happen overnight. In fact, I'm sure I'll be a perpetual student of communication. However, a wonderful aspect about communication is that you don't have to be born with it: this skill can be taught and learned. Better yet, with practice, great communication will be as simple as breathing – coming naturally without you even being conscious of it.

Let's begin by reviewing a few scenarios you might have encountered in your career.

Have you ever participated in or led a meeting where you felt those in the meeting were having their own meeting, or that you weren't able to achieve what you had hoped to get done?

Have you ever delivered a presentation to a large group and felt as though everyone was staring at you, and what you had rehearsed the night before (which seemed to go so well) suddenly felt awkward and unnatural?

Have you ever attempted to establish a connection with someone at work with whom you needed to collaborate closely, but even after months of trying, you were not able to form a solid working relationship?

Have you ever tried to implement a change, but despite all your work on the communications strategy, the people involved met the change with negativity, resistance and general inaction?

Have you ever wished you had more confidence in yourself? Would you like to manage your negative thoughts and deal better with conflicts as they arise?

These scenarios have one thing in common: they all have to do with *how you communicate*. And how you communicate in each of these situations will ultimately determine whether your voice is heard and remembered, or whether it's muffled in the noise that always surrounds our everyday lives. *Finding your voice in these situations will help you in your career.* Meetings, presentations, networking, change management and self-talk present what I call proof points in communication. Each of these proof points presents an opportunity to shine in front of others.

So what are you waiting for?
This is your time to shine!

"Life isn't about waiting for permission to be great. Seize the moment, bask in the rays of sunshine and simply shine."

— Anonymous

It's about to get a whole lot brighter!

My name is Gerry. And I am a communications advocate.

My experience in financial services, media, corporate training, international facilitation and now running my own communications business has taught me some of the best lessons in how to be a good communicator. Or, rather, lessons in how to shine.

We live in a time where "fast-paced" is considered slow and where impressions are often made before you get to say one single word. Let's face it: We live in a world that is quick to judge and slow to forgive. Just to be heard – let alone shine – may seem impossible.

However, please don't let this intimidate you on your ability to shine. It has never intimidated me. Not because I have an abundant supply of self-confidence or bravado, but because after all these years (and in more than 40 countries) of meetings, presentations and communications with people at all levels and industries – in support services, sales, executive roles and even leadership of countries – I can share with you some of the common traps you can fall into when communicating, and show you how to avoid them. I will also share insights into people and what they feel is important to them when being communicated to. Avoiding the traps of communication and knowing what people look for when you are communicating with them will help you achieve the following:

*You will be **heard**.*
*You will be **understood**.*
*You will have an **impact**.*
*You will have a **voice**.*
*You will be **remembered**, and most importantly,*
*You will **shine!***

Where to Shine: Communication Proof Points

Earlier, I used the term "proof points." This term originally comes from the marketing industry. Proof points refer to evidence to support a claim of value made about your product, your company or your service. That's a marketing proof point.

For our purposes, when talking about communication, I turn this concept around slightly. I believe communication proof points are evidence that support your claim of the value of *you*, and of your personal brand. Yes, how you communicate is part of your brand.

A brand is a promise. When you think about your personal brand, what does this mean? Well, for starters, how do people describe you? What do people say about you when you're not in the room? How do you want people to remember you?

Since the proof points are cornerstones of your personal brand, we're going to devote a section of the book to each of them.

In the section Brighter Meetings, we look at the *"Four Sins of Meetings."* What are the common pitfalls of these gatherings? How do we maximize each meeting, help people feel they've made progress and ensure they have had an effect on the outcomes? Having brighter meetings will demonstrate your ability to mobilize teams, move actions towards completion and effectively lead a project from kick-off to closure.

In Brighter Presentations, we look at where most presenters fail, including what goes wrong and how to avoid such presentation disasters as nerves, boring content, audience zombification and presenter lack of energy. Having brighter presentations will demonstrate your ability to deliver with conviction and confidence, command the attention of your audience and move them to action.

In Brighter Tomorrows, we look at why change communication can be challenging and how by understanding change through the eyes of those affected, we are better able to touch their hearts and minds and guide them through change successfully. Communicating and leading people to *Brighter Tomorrows* demonstrates your ability to manage conflict and deal with potentially difficult situations. When change communication is done well, the impact on people, customers and the organization's bottom line will be positive – and so will how others see you as a leader of change.

In Brighter Connections and Relationships, we look at the building blocks of creating successful business relationships. We'll examine how simple – yet often neglected – practices such as smiling, remembering someone's name, being interested and building loyal relationships could make the difference between "someone" sitting across the boardroom table from you and a "partner" who is there with you to get the job done! Securing *Brighter Connections and Relationships* demonstrates your ability to foster a collaborative environment that leverages creativity and skill sets. Creating a strong network of trusted relationships ultimately determines the height of your success.

In the final section, Brighter Thoughts, we examine your strongest opponent and ally to success: you. How can you increase your confidence, manage your 3 a.m. wake-up and worry episodes, travel beyond the borders of your comfort zone and tackle conflicts in a healthy and productive manner? Having *Brighter Thoughts* ultimately frames how you perceive your life. Did you know that how you look at life is often how life turns out for you? Your positive attitude attracts others to you because you represent someone they want to associate with!

An Invitation for You

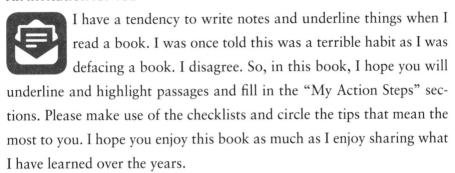 I have a tendency to write notes and underline things when I read a book. I was once told this was a terrible habit as I was defacing a book. I disagree. So, in this book, I hope you will underline and highlight passages and fill in the "My Action Steps" sections. Please make use of the checklists and circle the tips that mean the most to you. I hope you enjoy this book as much as I enjoy sharing what I have learned over the years.

I wish you a career that shines!

Did you know?

Z Z Z Z

39%
of meeting participants
admitted to dozing off
during a meeting

It is estimated that
25-50%
of meeting time is wasted

Source: www.meetingking.com/37-billion-per-year-unnecessary-meetings-share/

Brighter Meetings

"If you have to identify, in one word, the reason the human race has not achieved – and never will achieve – its full potential, that word would be meetings."

— Dave Barry, American humourist and author

Brighter Meetings:
How to Make them Efficient, Productive and Effective

Do you feel you attend too many meetings?

Do you feel many of them are unproductive and repetitive?

Have you ever attended a *Groundhog Day*[1] meeting where you say to yourself: "Haven't we talked about these exact same topics before?"

I average anywhere from four to six work-related meetings a day, not including conference calls, which I'll discuss a little later. And because my meetings are not limited to North American companies, but also include global organizations, I have the incredible advantage of learning by being a participant in those meetings, too. People in other countries have the same problems with meeting overload as we do.

For me, meetings are a way to move forward, create excitement, get things done, make key decisions and also connect with others, learn about each other and bring whatever you're working on to life.

The next time you run a meeting, ask yourself: Am I able to do the above? If not, reflect on what parts of your meetings are not working. What "meeting

---

[1] In case you haven't seen it, *Groundhog Day* is a hilarious movie in which Bill Murray portrays a weather reporter who lives the same day (February 2) over and over again.

sins" are you guilty of, and more importantly, what adjustments can you make that would have others say at the end of your meeting, "That was a really good meeting," "We were so productive at this meeting" or "Why can't all my meetings be like this one?"

Meetings are powerful, and your ability to be known for running productive meetings will get you noticed by others. So how can you have better meetings where attendees get what they need, feel a sense of accomplishment and are confident that work is progressing as it should? In other words, how can you shine in meetings?

Gerry's Tip

The best way to have more productive, efficient and effective meetings is to start by examining what often goes wrong in your meetings.

I find the best way to have more productive, efficient and effective meetings is to start by examining what often goes wrong. For me, it's easier to pick out what fails and then look at how to fix it. I call these the "The Four Sins of Meetings."

The Four Sins of Meetings

Sin #1: Wastefulness

Sin #2: Disorderly Conduct

Sin #3: Lateness

Sin #4: Disengagement

Sin #1: Wastefulness

John's Story

John has been attending his department's weekly meeting since he joined the company two and half years ago. These meetings tend to last an hour, sometimes longer. Everyone has to share what they are working on and how things are progressing. John always ends up going last because he usually has the least to say. Not because he is doing less work, but unlike his teammates who make sure every detail of their assignments is aired and acknowledged, John just wants to let his supervisor know that all is going according to plan, or to alert him if he needs help with any aspect of the project. John often wonders why others on the team feel the need to go into great detail about what they are working on and how they are making a difference. He often leaves these meetings feeling both frustrated and somewhat inadequate compared to his teammates.

What John feels is not uncommon, because we have become ritualistic in the way we organize meetings. Wastefulness in meetings isn't so much about the hours or minutes spent but more about what is being done during this time. Although meetings can be important and do serve a purpose, what we actually do during meetings is what makes them wasteful.

So how do we make our meetings more meaningful? These questions will lead you in the right direction and help you be seen as an effective meeting co-ordinator.

Question #1: Do we need to meet?

Here are five really good reasons to meet:

1. **Make decisions** – The group must table ideas and options where a decision needs to be made in order to move forward.

2. **Generate ideas** – The group needs to brainstorm a lot of ideas and to generate some creative ideas.

3. **Share progress and updates** – The group needs to update and share information with others in order to move forward.

4. **Deliver information** – The group needs to hear from individuals about communication that affects them and to have the opportunity to address questions.

5. **Make a plan** – The group needs to outline a plan of action.

Question #2: How long do we need to meet?

Here are some principles I always keep in mind regarding attention span and information absorption when planning my meetings:

1. Adults have about a 20-minute attention span before their minds begin to wander.[2]

2. People learn best given a variety of visual, audio and tactile content.

3. Individuals all need expectations of them to be set; structure is important.

4. We need time to reflect and ask questions for clarification.

Consider the above principles when planning how much time you need for your meeting. Again, it is not so much the *amount* of time that makes meetings wasteful. In fact, if there is sufficient structure, a variety of delivery formats (visual, audio and tactile), topics that are to the point, and an opportunity to ask questions, no one will complain about the length of the meeting. It's when these principles are neglected that meetings become boring, redundant and wasteful.

Gerry's Tip

Do not be constrained by intervals of 30 minutes. Some of the most effective and meaningful meetings I've experienced are shorter than 20 minutes.

Here's one final note about how much time to plan for your meeting: do not be constrained by intervals of 30 minutes. Some of the most effective and meaningful meetings I've experienced are shorter than 20 minutes. In fact, an executive for whom I have an incredible amount of admiration sets her meetings to 10 minutes. Yes, you must be organized, but let me tell you: These meetings work, and by the end of the allotted time, everyone knows what is needed to move forward.

The next time you plan a meeting, see what you can do to shave 10 to 15 minutes off the time. If you traditionally hold hour-long meetings, try setting one for 45 minutes and let people know upfront what you are doing. They will help you! Think about the material that needs to be sent ahead of time, and what can be accomplished by email. By shaving minutes off your meetings, you will become more efficient with your time – and that of participants – and this will be noticed and appreciated.

Question #3: Do we need to meet every week?

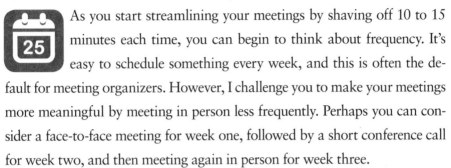 As you start streamlining your meetings by shaving off 10 to 15 minutes each time, you can begin to think about frequency. It's easy to schedule something every week, and this is often the default for meeting organizers. However, I challenge you to make your meetings more meaningful by meeting in person less frequently. Perhaps you can consider a face-to-face meeting for week one, followed by a short conference call for week two, and then meeting again in person for week three.

The sequence is not important. What's important is thinking about how much time people need to actually sit face-to-face with one another to get things done. Remember that meetings can become ritualistic and it's easy to fall into meeting-cycle habits. Fine-tuning your meetings means really thinking about these questions, and being aware of the attention span and focus principles I mentioned, along with a healthy dose of trial and error. Regardless of how you end up – and maybe it doesn't change your meeting frequencies – the fact you are thinking about *how* to make your meetings more meaningful and not wasteful will inevitably make them more efficient, effective and productive. Being respectful of people's time and schedules is always a plus in my book. And having worked in so many different organizations, I can tell you that if you can help people find time in their day, you will be a star!

Let's discuss the next meeting sin and how we can fix it: *Disorderly Conduct.*

Sin #2: Disorderly Conduct

Have you ever felt a meeting you organized was anything but yours? Do you sometimes feel one topic seems to monopolize a meeting and nothing else gets done? Have you finished a meeting where there is still no end in sight for solving important issues and people are leaving frustrated?

Shannon's Story

Shannon felt ready for her kick-off meeting with the steering committee. Before the meeting, she prepared handouts of the cost spreadsheets for her upcoming conference, along with a tentative project plan as well as pictures of the proposed location for the event. She even had a high-level agenda with three topics: location, budget and project plan.

The committee, which was charged with making key decisions, included a number of Shannon's colleagues, supervisors and the unit heads. Shannon made sure she invited as many people as possible to this meeting to gather their input and ideas. After all, the more people, the more ideas, she thought. The meeting started at 9 a.m. and everyone arrived on time. After a bit of chitchat about the traffic, last evening's snowstorm, and of course checking last-minute messages on their devices, Shannon started the meeting by thanking everyone for coming. She was surprised everyone showed up but was happy to see it was now standing-room-only in their modest-sized boardroom. She began to say there were three things she wanted to discuss today: location, budget and project plan. In fact, she'd hoped to cover all three in the hour set aside for this meeting.

Suddenly Shannon's colleague, Amanda, jumped in and started talking about an amazing event her husband had held at a wonderful venue just north of the city. She went on to describe the activities they did at this event, the rooms and the spa services. "We should really look into this place!" she said. Her supervisor, Tracy, said she too had heard great things about it. "But I heard it was pricey," piped in Manuel, one of Shannon's supervisors, who added, "But we should still explore it since our event is only once a year and is a real booster for the sales team." Then he asked Shannon to share the budget plans.

Shannon switched gears quickly in her head from what she had prepared to say about the locations, and then started fumbling with her budget papers. As soon as she began to share numbers, questions poured in from everyone: "How come this was so expensive?" "Do we need to spend money for gift bags?" "What were we planning for the gift bags?" "Do people even use their gift bags?"

Glancing at her BlackBerry, Shannon was shocked to see it was already 9:55 and people were beginning to exit for their next meeting. Sam, the unit head, was the first to leave. He didn't say a word throughout the meeting, other than as he was leaving: "Sounds like you've got a lot of work ahead of you, Shannon. You probably need to have more meetings."

Within minutes, everyone had left the room and Shannon sat there with her handouts in paper clips and her laptop with all the venue options still facing her. She felt as though nothing she wanted to achieve was done and now she'd have to schedule another meeting with everyone.

What Shannon experienced happens more often than we realize. It's frustrating not only because you don't get what you want out of the meeting, but also because your participants don't walk away any closer to where they wanted to go.

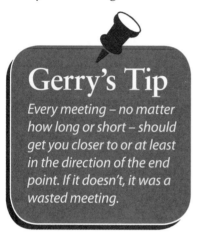

Gerry's Tip

Every meeting – no matter how long or short – should get you closer to or at least in the direction of the end point. If it doesn't, it was a wasted meeting.

Having clear objectives – what you want to get out of the meeting, and to get from participants and decision-makers – is your best defence against what I call "disorderly conduct." What happened to Shannon was not anyone's fault, and no one was trying to sabotage her meeting. People can easily be distracted at meetings. Keep in mind you don't know what's in their heads when they walk in. Have they come from an intense meeting where they had to present, or have they just finished a difficult call with a colleague or client? Are they preoccupied with something they are working on and consider your meeting an interruption to their day? Everyone is entitled to have things going on in their heads. We all do. So the sooner you are clear on exactly what you want from participants at the meeting, the more efficient and effective you will become.

Setting objectives doesn't have to be difficult. I usually start by asking myself one question before I even plan the agenda. It could be as simple as:

- **By the end of this meeting, what do I want to happen? OR**

- **What do I need to have by the end of this meeting to move forward?**

Since you are asking this only of yourself, just let the answer pour out, but write it down. This will form the first draft of your objective for your meeting. Now here's the really important part: Objectives need to be shared at the start of the meeting.

If you don't share your objectives, participants will not know how to help you get there. And all they will do is "contribute" their ideas and thoughts. While this is all well intended, remember what happened to Shannon! Imagine what would have happened if Shannon had instead started off her meeting with the following:

"Thanks everyone for coming. We have one hour to go through three key items. And while an hour may not be enough to go through each one in detail, here's what I'd like to achieve with your help:

- **Location** – I want to share three with you that fit our budget and have received very good reviews from previous attendees.

- **Budget** – I will share with you five components that make up the bulk of our budget. The purpose is for everyone to understand where money gets spent.

- **Project plan** – I will share the seven areas of our plan and want you to think about those areas you would like to have a role in. Based on that, we will form seven smaller working groups which will meet independently and come together as a larger group only when updates are needed.

These three items will take me no more than 25 minutes to present and then we can discuss each in more detail and share your ideas in the second part of the meeting. Is everyone all right with this format? I do want to hear from you, but would like to first present all my findings so you have the entire picture of what we need to accomplish today."

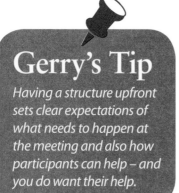

Gerry's Tip

Having a structure upfront sets clear expectations of what needs to happen at the meeting and also how participants can help – and you do want their help.

While people may still have questions and comments throughout the meeting, Shannon has set the stage for how she would like the meeting to run. And for the most part, people will agree to this format knowing they will have a chance to voice their opinions. Having a structure like this upfront sets clear expectations of what needs to happen at the meeting and also how participants can help – and you do want their help. Participation is key. However, in meetings with limited time and with more than one topic, you need structure.

Being prepared in advance for a meeting is essential for successful and brighter meetings. While there is an investment of time, it is not a huge commitment. And the investment of just 20 to 30 minutes of planning is almost guaranteed to increase your success rate.

Now that you have the outcomes or objectives (what you want to achieve from this meeting), you can develop your agenda, including those items or topics that need to be covered for you to reach those objectives.

Six Ideas for Agenda Setting

 While there are no hard and fast rules for setting good agendas, here are some tips I have learned from holding as well as attending meetings over the years:

1. *Divide your agenda into two parts.* The top half contains items you MUST get through; the bottom half, while important, is of lower priority and can move to another meeting if needed.

2. *Have a clear "ask"* after each agenda item. Something like this:
   - Agenda topic: Theme of event – Need to agree and decide on the theme

3. *Use sub-bullets to help guide and keep participants focused:*
   - Agenda topic: Meals
     » Breakfast – Buffet style or voucher
     » Working lunches – Boxed or buffet
     » Dinners – Hotel or external location

4. At the top of the agenda, *list the objectives* you want to reach by the end of the meeting. This will help guide the meeting and keep things on track.

5. *Leave lots of space between agenda items for people to write notes.* This will help them remember action items (I will talk more about this later) and will be an easy take-away for them to keep them informed of what happened at the meeting.

6. With objectives and an agenda in hand, one last preparation I like to do before meetings (once I know a meeting is needed and an email or conference call is not sufficient), is something called *MAPIT.* This

becomes a mental roadmap that helps guide your meetings. MAPIT, an invention of mine, stands for:

MAPIT

MEMBERS
ACTION ITEMS
PRIORITIES
IDENTIFY LEADERS
TIMING

Gerry's Tip

Too many people in your initial meetings can cause disinterest among participants. Include only those members you feel are absolutely necessary.

MEMBERS

In order to reach the objectives you set out, you need to have the right people at the table. Remember Shannon? She invited everyone in her unit to attend. While this was a very inclusive gesture and would have been good at some point, it was not appropriate for her initial meeting, given her objectives. With too many people, you get too many opinions. Think about the five types of meetings, and ask yourself: Who NEEDS to be at this meeting?

1. **Make decisions** – The group must table ideas and options where a decision needs to be made in order to move forward.

2. **Generate ideas** – The group needs to brainstorm a lot of ideas and to generate some creative ideas.

3. **Share progress and updates** – The group needs to update and share information with others in order to move forward.

4. **Deliver information** – The group needs to hear from individuals about communication that affects them and to have the opportunity to address questions.

5. **Make a plan** – The group needs to outline a plan of action.

6. **Invite the right people** – If you need to make a decision and the decision-maker is not present, you won't accomplish what you set out to do.

If you have a decision to make, be sure the decision-maker is in the room.

If you wish to brainstorm, bring in as many people as you can. The more the merrier.

If you need to strategize, bring in leaders who can help lead the strategy.

If you need to inform, bring in people who can help you create a meaningful and appropriate communication.

If you must provide status updates, bring in people who are actually doing the work and can share their updates with you.

The above seems almost too simple to mess up, but believe me, having the wrong members present is common and is one of the real reasons why meetings are ineffective and inefficient.

ACTION ITEMS

Action items are critical to demonstrate progress towards an end point. Without action items, there is no stake in the ground to prove you are moving forward. Once an action has been decided on, you have made progress. Simple as that. **Progress is the name of the game when it comes to good meetings.**

I am a big believer in holding people accountable for what they said or what they were asked to do. We don't hold people accountable often enough. At the end, decide what will happen in the next meeting. Be sure each person is accountable for following through on what they were supposed to do. A simple "action items email" can go out that same day, listing people's names and specific tasks for the next meeting.

I have found it very effective to share that same list of action items just before the next meeting. I call this book-ending accountability. After the meeting, I am clear on what I need to do; and just before the next meeting, I am reminded that I am scheduled to present my findings. If people cannot attend the next meeting, be sure they send you their findings so you can share. *Not attending a meeting is not an excuse to not complete the action item.*

Accountability is a funny thing. Once people have committed to doing something and see their name next to it, it is very difficult to escape, so the group becomes self-governing. The key is to let them know before the meeting ends that they will receive an email immediately after the meeting to remind everyone of the action items, then one just before the next meeting to remind them of their role at the meeting. Action items move things forward.

PRIORITIES

Despite our best intentions to cover all items on the agenda, it can be challenging. Some topics take up more time than expected. The rule I follow when it comes to extended discussions on a topic is this: If this discussion is going to lead me to achieve the objective I need from this meeting, I will let it continue, because I

Gerry's Tip

Setting priorities helps ensure you get what you need out of the meeting. Put "must-cover" topics on the top half of your agenda.

need an outcome. If, however, it is not directly related to something I need to achieve, I simply say, "Let's take this offline." Sometimes, just a short intervention like this is all that's needed to move on. The others will thank you for speaking up!

Setting priorities helps ensure you get what you need out of the meeting. Earlier I mentioned that the top half of your agenda should list the "must-cover" topics and the bottom half as "important, but not critical." This helps you get what you need most from the meeting, and if topics are left uncovered, it does not hamper your ability to keep moving forward.

IDENTIFYING LEADERS

Participant engagement is another important indicator of good meetings. I talk about engagement later on in this chapter, but for now, as we prepare for our meetings, think of members who can act as leaders on various topics and tasks. This accomplishes a number of things – namely, the sharing of accountability. Having ownership engages people, and when you have the right people who can contribute to something you're working on, everyone wins.

While facilitating a workshop in Pretoria, South Africa, I learned about identifying leaders, and having different leaders at your meetings. There's a really good reason for this. First of all, you don't need all the work to be on *your* shoulders! If you are responsible for all the preparation, slides (if you're using them), printing, doing all the speaking, getting consensus, etc., it can be overwhelming. To counter this, the people I met in South Africa use a concept called "share the chair" – letting someone else lead the meeting, or just a portion of it. This allows someone else to develop his or her ability to run a meeting.

At the same time, *you* get to be an observer of the meeting. Think of the benefits of sharing the chair: When you're not responsible for all the talking, you can do more listening. You can better observe how the meeting is really going. Is it working? Share the chair, if you want to keep the dynamics of your meetings moving and if you need to develop people's meeting skills.

TIMING

Stay on time. Simple as that! Timing is very important for meetings. How upset are you when you're asked to come to a meeting, you've been pushed out another half-hour, and now you're late for your other commitments? When you keep to your time, or better yet, end a few minutes early (say 10 minutes early) you're showing that you're efficient with your time and that you are a productive chair.

Keeping time starts with the agenda. Having too many items on there will guarantee you will run out of time. Using sub-bullets on the agenda will help since it will direct you to your objectives.

Having someone call time for each section is also helpful. The key is to move to the next topic but have some closure on the current one. For example, have someone to take "next steps" on this specific item and report back at the next meeting (Note: this would then be an action item).

Keeping time means you are respectful of participants' time. Time is an extremely valuable resource and minutes count. See people's reaction the next time you end a meeting five to 10 minutes early. You will be appreciated more than you realize!

Setting objectives, creating a well-planned agenda, and preparing ahead using MAPIT will help you prevent "disorderly conduct" at meetings. Instead, you will run more structured, focused and results-oriented sessions, and people *will* notice!

Sin #3: Lateness

Have you ever had to re-start a meeting because attendees arrived late? Have you ever lost your train of thought or the flow of a meeting as a result of late arrivals?

Ahmad's Story

Ahmad looked at his BlackBerry and saw the time was 2:07 p.m. This was only supposed to be a 30-minute update meeting about their upcoming marketing materials. Most of the people were there except for his supervisor, Jane, who tended to be late for all his meetings. He was torn whether to start or not but could tell people were beginning to get restless and doing their own thing on their various devices. At 2:11 p.m. he finally decided to start. His agenda was brief: Showcase three marketing materials designs, get feedback on which one the group favored, and share the timing and details of the launch at the end of the month.

Ahmad was making good time despite the late start. He was able to get through the designs and get good feedback on what the group liked, as well as changes that needed to be made. At 2:23 p.m. he was about to move to the final item on his agenda, which was the timing of the launch and impact on each department, when Jane rushed in. Apologizing for being late, she looked around the room hoping to assess where people were with the design selections. "Sorry folks," she said. "What a day so far! So, Ahmad, what did I miss?"

"We just finished the design of the marketing materials, got everyone's feedback and were just about to cover the launch details," Ahmad said.

"Oh," Jane said, "I really wanted to hear what the group thought. What did everyone think about the three designs?"

The meeting finally ended at 3:10 p.m., 40 minutes longer than his invitation stated. Everyone now was running late as they hurried back to their offices.

Four Ways to Stay on Track

Lateness is something that we all confront within business. There is always something to make us late. Sometimes we are the culprits or, as in the above scenario, others can set us back. A golden rule of meetings: Start on time, end on time (or early)! Here are some steps to avoid the problems caused by lateness.

For example, when someone arrives late at your meeting, the worst thing to do is to update him or her on what they missed. The other people in the room then have to sit there and listen to your recap. Everyone's time needs to be respected, and this will be seen as a reflection of how efficient you are (or are not).

Here are some ways to help you avoid the problems caused by lateness:

1. Be Known for Being Punctual

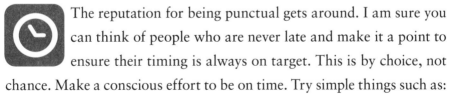 The reputation for being punctual gets around. I am sure you can think of people who are never late and make it a point to ensure their timing is always on target. This is by choice, not chance. Make a conscious effort to be on time. Try simple things such as:

- Leave 10 minutes earlier for meetings

- Account for unplanned delays

- Don't start something you know will take more time than you have; even a few minutes could expand unexpectedly.

Examples:

- Responding "quickly" to an email

- Answering a call

- Stopping by someone's desk or office "just for a minute"

- Grabbing a coffee

These may seem like minor "time offenses" but we've all experienced being delayed by others. Nobody likes that feeling.

2. Just Start the Meeting

 I remember that university professors would start their lectures with or without everyone in the room. The same rule applies here. In the scenario above, Ahmad was torn because it was his supervisor who was running late and he felt he needed to wait for her. However, he could have done a couple of things differently. First, start on time. At 2:00 p.m., he could have begun the meeting, and instead of going through the designs and feedback session first, he could have covered off some logistical items related to the launch timing. Assuming his supervisor Jane needed to be there for the design feedback, if Ahmad had moved the agenda items slightly, he could have kept things on time. The other option would be to let Jane know when she arrived that he had captured all the feedback, and he could stay behind to share them with her after the meeting.

3. Keep it Moving

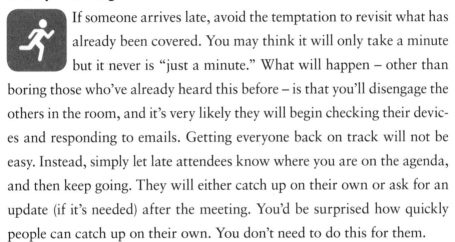 If someone arrives late, avoid the temptation to revisit what has already been covered. You may think it will only take a minute but it never is "just a minute." What will happen – other than boring those who've already heard this before – is that you'll disengage the others in the room, and it's very likely they will begin checking their devices and responding to emails. Getting everyone back on track will not be easy. Instead, simply let late attendees know where you are on the agenda, and then keep going. They will either catch up on their own or ask for an update (if it's needed) after the meeting. You'd be surprised how quickly people can catch up on their own. You don't need to do this for them.

4. End on Time

Always have some way to let everyone know what time it is. Use such verbal indicators as "We have 10 minutes left and I want to make sure we cover off this last item" or "In the last five minutes, I want to address any questions you have before we end this meeting." This will let attendees know you are keeping a close eye on time and will be ending on time. Being vocal about how much time is left is a very good way to set the tone throughout the meeting. You will find that people will work with you to finish on time. There is nothing worse than ending a meeting and hearing people say: "Oh, I didn't know it was this late already!"

If you place the most important items at the top half of your agenda, when you run behind schedule you can move uncovered items to the bottom of the agenda for the *next* meeting. Having a good sense of what *must* be covered will ensure you address key areas so you can keep your project moving forward.

Being punctual at meetings – starting on time, not wasting time to "recap" for latecomers, and ending on time – projects to others that you are in control of both the agenda and time. This, in turn, reflects on your ability to manage time well, guide people effectively and manage disruption with confidence, all of which leaves a great impression on others!

Sin #4: Disengagement

Have you ever held a meeting where the only person fully engaged was you? Have you tried to seek input or feedback but heard only silence from the group? Has it ever been painful – "like pulling teeth" – when you tried to create some dialogue or discussion on something you need input on?

Jason's Story

"Does anyone have any questions?" Jason asked as he looked around the boardroom. But only blank stares and averted looks greeted him. He had been presenting his status updates for about 20 minutes and was about to move to the next agenda item, but felt he should ask for questions or feedback. After all, this was a working committee and they should have input into how things were progressing.

He first looked to Cyndi, who usually has a comment to share, but noticed she was thumbing her BlackBerry, probably responding to an email or text. "OK, then, let's move on to ideas for the theme of this event. Who has some ideas for a theme?" Again, silence. Luckily, Bob piped up and said: "Well, I thought it might be good to go with a heroes theme this year."

"OK, that's good," said Jason. "Anyone else like that idea – and how we can build on it?" Only disinterested and "Oh God, please don't pick on me" looks came back to Jason. "What about other ideas? You must have some you can share?"

Jason looked at his watch and saw there were only a few minutes left in this meeting anyway, so he asked them all to think about themes for the next meeting. Everyone nodded their heads as they happily packed up their folders and left.

Jason had hoped they would be more engaged, since everyone's role had been assigned and this was already their second meeting together.

Getting People Engaged

Great meetings have always reminded me of one of my favourite activities as a kid – Lego. Like Lego, great meetings have ideas that build off one another, and the possibilities become limitless. In fact, you know you have a great and engaged meeting when you feel inspired afterwards from talking and sharing ideas. It's a good feeling and one that often propels progress and gets everyone excited about the eventual outcome.

Getting people engaged, however, is not often easy. You know this is true, because we have all spent far too many meetings being comfortable as passive participants. Have no fear, though, because this *is* reversible, and I'm going to share a few techniques I have used successfully to transform even the most disengaged person into an active and enthusiastic participant.

Eight Engagement Techniques

Gerry's Tip

Play is great for engaging people. When we shift our minds out of work mode and play – even just for a few minutes – our ideas flow much better.

1. Happy Hands, Active Minds

I once read that the company 3M, which I consider one of the most creative companies producing some of the most useful, interesting and innovative products in the market today, uses this technique to get people more creative and engaged. At their meetings, they provide items for people to play with. Yes, play. When we shift our minds out of work mode and play – even just for a few minutes – our ideas flow much better.

"Play" is one of my personal mantras when it comes to engaging people. We live and work around urgent deadlines and unending revisions of documentation. This can create what I refer to as zombified employees. The antidote is to bring them back to a time where life was much simpler and more fun.

At the next meeting where you need people to be creative or have good discussions, try the following items, all of which can easily be found at your local dollar store:

- Squeeze balls

- Silly Putty

- Play-Doh

- Colourful magic markers

These are just a few of the items I've used with great success. The options are limitless when you start thinking in the direction of "play," so I hope you'll have some fun here.

As people enter the room, they will notice these items and most likely just pick them up and start using them. Encourage this, but don't say it's to make them more creative. Just invite them to have fun with the items. In my experience, most people gravitate towards them without much encouragement, but it depends on your group. You will notice that people begin talking about the last time they saw these items, and this instantly changes the mood in the room from "just another meeting" to "cool meeting!"

2. Set Expectations

This seems obvious, but it's very important to let people know what you want and what you expect of them at the meeting. A good way to accomplish this is to send a short (and I repeat *short*) email with a few bullet points about what you need them to bring to the meeting. I stressed the word "short" because I have seen many email reminders where there are charts, attachments and paragraphs of information trying to set expectations. The reality is that most people will simply read the first few lines, and if it takes too much effort to digest the information, they will not read the rest. Here's an example of what I would consider a good reminder email:

To: Ahmad, Shannon, John

Cc:

Subject: Today's Meeting

Hi everyone. Just a quick "ask" for our meeting this afternoon:

1. Bring three of your favourite songs you feel would be high energy for our event.

2. Based on last year's event: What MUST we do again? What should we PASS on?

3. Tag lines you think we should consider for this year's event.

Thanks and see you at 2 p.m. – Ocean View room (6th floor)

3. Move Me

I attended a meeting once where each participant received a series of sticker dots (red, green and blue). These stickers are easy to find at any stationery store and even most dollar stores. When participants entered the meeting, they saw along the wall flipchart paper with topics written across the top.

Gerry's Tip

Getting people to move around during a meeting is a great way to engage, energize and elevate participants' level of involvement.

Participants were asked to place a green dot on the topics they felt were most important to them and should be on the agenda for the upcoming off-site event. A blue dot indicated important but not mandatory, and a red dot for topics they felt were not important.

This exercise of selecting the importance of topics could also have been done with a raising of hands (a more common way). But this dot approach created something unique that would not have been done with the raising of hands. It made people move around the room. This always creates more energy. As well, people started discussing their selections with one another, which created dialogue and which offered an early indication of where the group was headed. By the time everyone completed their selections, the buzz in the room was high, and asking people for their rationale and feedback was a breeze. Getting people to move around during a meeting is a great way to engage, energize and elevate participants' level of involvement.

4. Music

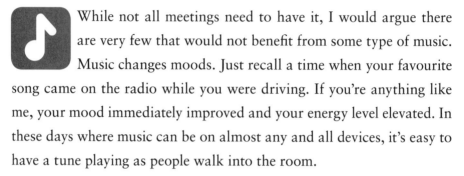

While not all meetings need to have it, I would argue there are very few that would not benefit from some type of music. Music changes moods. Just recall a time when your favourite song came on the radio while you were driving. If you're anything like me, your mood immediately improved and your energy level elevated. In these days where music can be on almost any and all devices, it's easy to have a tune playing as people walk into the room.

What I've learned from running meetings where music was used, either as people entered or as part of the meeting itself (e.g., selecting songs for an event), you will undoubtedly see an increase in energy and entertainment value. Do not underestimate this technique. The ability to change moods is a powerful tool to get the most out of people and to have effective meetings. There's an added bonus when people feel better after the meeting because you have been able to lift their mood. *You* are the one responsible for this – not a bad way for people to think about you!

5. Food

Depending on the time you schedule your meeting, you could be hosting some people who are famished because they have missed lunch. Now when I say "food," I don't mean meals! Snacks might be a better way to describe this. Whenever I screen a video with a client, I always try to bring popcorn because it's an association people make with movies. So when they screen my video, they associate it with something pleasurable as well as tasty! Other items I have used in the past with much success include licorice, Tic Tacs and Pez. Whatever you decide to share or serve, make it easy to eat and, if possible, fun. Childhood items or snacks they don't normally get will always create more interest. Other than being fun, a boost of sugar is good for creativity and energy.

6. Sticky Notes

 Brainstorming can be challenging, especially when you're starting a meeting. Try this next time you need to get the flow started. During one of my strategy sessions to improve a process for an IT company, I told everyone they had one minute to write down all the challenges they currently had with the existing process. The rule was to write each challenge on a sticky note, so there should be 10 or more at the end of the minute. After this exercise was done, I told them they had another minute to write down 10 quick fixes we could explore to solve the process issue.

Within the first five minutes of the meeting, I had eight senior level managers fully engaged and more than 80 ideas for possible solutions. Yes, many were similar, but by the end of the meeting, we had 10 solid ideas to pursue and present to the leadership team.

Being creative in getting ideas out of people is what will differentiate you from others when it comes to brainstorming. Be creative, make it easy and make it fun. This is my formula for success that has served me well for many years.

7. Crayons

 Just for fun, next time you have a meeting where people need to write down ideas or contribute during the meeting, replace their pens with Crayola crayons. Get a giant box (or two) and place it in the centre of the table. Watch what happens. Have fun with this idea. It will bring out the inner child in everyone, and as you recall from childhood, the inner child has some of the most imaginative and creative ideas of all – ideas that are not self-censored or dismissed too early.

8. "Do you have any questions?"

This is perhaps the most common question asked during meetings to gain understanding, acceptance and possible agreement. Often, though, this question is met with either silence or little response. The reason I don't like this question (not to say it should not be used – just not as the first one) is that before adults will ask a question, they need reflection, which requires time. And because of the time needed to think of questions, there are usually long pauses – and we all know how we love long pauses when we're in front of an audience.

> **Gerry's Tip**
>
> The best times for meetings are Tuesday, Wednesday and Thursday either mid-morning or early afternoon.

I have always found asking *"How does what I shared with you make you feel?"* to be much more effective at getting a response. People will have a much more immediate reaction (how they feel about something) than they do direct questions. From getting to how they feel, you can dig deeper with *"What makes you feel that way?"* and so on. You'll find that using that one question will get you more insight as well as create a natural segue to other questions.

When is the best time to hold meetings?

 Research tells us something revealing about where people's heads are during the week. And this gives us insight into when might be the best times to have meetings.

Monday mornings: People are still in weekend mode and getting them to open up can be a challenge, because to them, it's still Sunday!

Friday afternoons: People are already in weekend mode. They are not prepared to invest what's needed, because the week has already drained whatever brain power they have.

The best times for meetings are *Tuesday, Wednesday* and *Thursday* either mid-morning or early afternoon. This is when people are in full work mode and the week has not yet gotten the better of them.

These techniques work to engage and involve participants at your meetings! Use them and trust them. Most importantly, have fun with them.

On my Gerry Lewis Inc. website *www.gerrylewis.com* I have this statement:

> *"Creating a sense of play is my secret weapon.*
> *I never apologize for my reliance on fun.*
>
> ---
>
> *It leads to the biggest ideas. It engages a team from day one.*
> *Energy goes up. Excitement builds. And, it helps the*
> *team connect the dots."*

Spotlight Conference calls:

Hello, is there anyone there?

"The single biggest problem in communication is the illusion that it has taken place."

— George Bernard Shaw, Irish author

Have you ever felt like you were the only person on the conference call?

Have you ever felt those long and painful pauses while trying to get others to speak on the call?

Have you ever had someone who would not stop talking on a call?

Paul's Story

Paul dialed into the conference call early. As the chair for this call, he wanted to make sure he was there to welcome everyone. This call was particularly important. His VP Mary, who was working this week in Hong Kong, had asked him to set up this call. After speaking with people in their offices in Hong Kong, Malaysia and Singapore, Mary noticed they felt disconnected from the Canadian office, and also from Paul, who was responsible for the off-site offices.

Their email exchanges had always been pleasant and productive, so Mary's request for the call was somewhat of a surprise to Paul. In this first call, his objective was to reassure these far-flung teams that they had a voice and their issues were being heard.

A number of beeps sounded, indicating people were signing into the call. After a few more beeps, Paul thanked everyone for staying late; there was a 10- to 12-hour time difference for this 7 a.m. call in Toronto. After some pleasantries – mostly by Paul – there was silence on the other end.

Paul proceeded with the agenda. There really was only one item: how to improve communication between these three offices and the Toronto office.

Paul started with some ideas about how to improve their communication and asked if anyone had any comments. Silence.

He asked if anyone thought the timeframes he proposed were manageable. A couple of voices bounced back with a soft "Yes, it's manageable." Paul thanked them, more as a way to kill the deafening silence than anything else.

Paul tried another approach by asking James, their Hong Kong lead, to contribute ideas. But when he asked James to say a few words, there was more silence. A voice finally responded. It was Anita from the Hong Kong office: "Sorry, Paul, but James had to miss the call due to a family situation today." Paul suddenly realized he wasn't sure who was or was not on the call and asked if everyone could identify themselves. After about 10 seconds of silence, which felt like an hour to Paul, all the voices seemed to jump online at the same time, making none of them audible or identifiable. "That didn't help much," Paul thought to himself.

The call continued for another 20 minutes, with much of the speaking done by Paul with a few "OK," "Sounds good" and "Yes, we will" responses. When Paul ended the call, he realized that Mary, his VP, was also on the line and asked Paul if he could call her afterwards for a debrief.

Gerry's Tip

Ideally, you want to make remote callers feel like they are in the same room as you.

My guiding principle on conference calls is this: Do not be ruled by the medium, as Paul was in the story above. One of your main objectives should be to draw remote people in, so they feel they are actually participating in the room.

Four Steps to Conference Call Success

Conference calls have become a business necessity and in many cases can be a very efficient way to conduct most types of meetings. Many, if not all, of the ideas shared so far apply to both face-to-face meetings and virtual ones (conference calls, video conferences, web conferences).

The challenge with virtual meetings is that you may not be able to see the others, making it difficult to gauge their level of attention and keep them engaged.

When I was working with international clients, conference calls were not just an option; it was the only way we could meet. Here are a few of my practices that will help make your conference calls more effective, engaging and efficient.

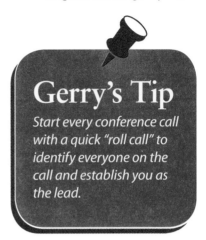

Gerry's Tip

Start every conference call with a quick "roll call" to identify everyone on the call and establish you as the lead.

1. Know Who's On the Call

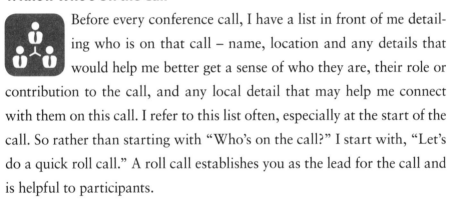

Before every conference call, I have a list in front of me detailing who is on that call – name, location and any details that would help me better get a sense of who they are, their role or contribution to the call, and any local detail that may help me connect with them on this call. I refer to this list often, especially at the start of the call. So rather than starting with "Who's on the call?" I start with, "Let's do a quick roll call." A roll call establishes you as the lead for the call and is helpful to participants.

2. Set Expectations

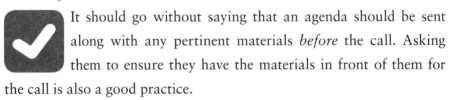

It should go without saying that an agenda should be sent along with any pertinent materials *before* the call. Asking them to ensure they have the materials in front of them for the call is also a good practice.

When I start the call, I again let them know they should have the materials in front of them. I also start the call with a very clear objective and the time we have for this call.

Setting expectations also means letting participants know how they can help you and provides them a process by which to do so.

3. Call People Out – With Plenty of Warning

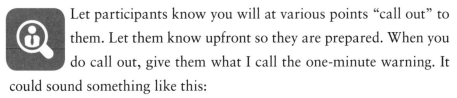 Let participants know you will at various points "call out" to them. Let them know upfront so they are prepared. When you do call out, give them what I call the one-minute warning. It could sound something like this:

> "So that's a look at our last quarter and what we need to reach for our next quarter. What I'd like to do now is to begin some call-outs for reaction and feasibility of these goals. I'll start with the farthest location and work my way in. John, can we start with you?"

When participants have warnings and clear instructions on what they are supposed to report on, you will find they are better prepared and more ready and willing to respond.

4. Share the Chair

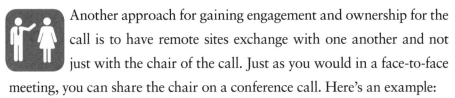 Another approach for gaining engagement and ownership for the call is to have remote sites exchange with one another and not just with the chair of the call. Just as you would in a face-to-face meeting, you can share the chair on a conference call. Here's an example:

> Paul had three offices on the call – Hong Kong, Malaysia and Singapore. What he could have done early in the call was to ask the three offices to provide their ideas on how to improve commu-

nication with Toronto. Following their responses, Paul could have invited the three cities to share what they do as regional offices from which they could all learn. This method would encourage the three offices to exchange and share what they do, while offering the chair the opportunity to take on the role of participant as well. "Sharing the chair" or shared leadership is not only a good method of engaging remote callers, it's also a great way to gain insight you may not have received if you led the entire call yourself.

Final Thoughts

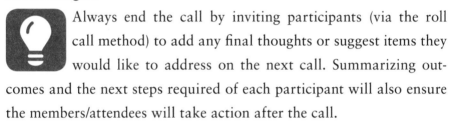 Always end the call by inviting participants (via the roll call method) to add any final thoughts or suggest items they would like to address on the next call. Summarizing outcomes and the next steps required of each participant will also ensure the members/attendees will take action after the call.

These small enhancements to your call will enable you to manage time, agenda and virtual participants with greater ease and confidence, thus ensuring a much more successful outcome.

Recap

The four sins of meetings

Sin #1: Wastefulness

Sin #2: Disorderly conduct

Sin #3: Lateness

Sin #4: Disengagement

Meeting checklist

☐ Do we need to meet?

☐ How long do we need to meet?

☐ Do we need to meet every week?

Five really good reasons to meet

1. Make decisions

2. Generate ideas

3. Update status and progress

4. Share information

5. Make a plan

Remember MAPIT

Members

Action items

Priorities

Identify leaders

Timing

The golden rule of meetings: start on time, end on time (or early!)

Be known for being punctual

Even if people are late, just start the meeting

Keep it moving

Always end on time

Eight engagement techniques

1. **Happy hands, active minds**

2. **Set expectations**

3. **Move me**

4. **Music**

5. Food

6. Sticky notes

7. Crayons

8. "Do you have any questions?"

Checklist for conference call success

☐ Know who's on the call

☐ Set expectations

☐ Call people out – with plenty of warning

☐ Share the chair

Ask Gerry

Q You mentioned that a meeting organizer needs to have clear objectives to conduct a successful meeting, but how do you deal with work colleagues who feel threatened by your success? Other people don't always want to give you an opportunity to shine, because they don't want to be surpassed on the corporate ladder. How do you deal with competitive colleagues in meetings?

A This can definitely happen but I also believe that excellence will always shine over office politics. If you don't get that opportunity to shine in front of others because people don't give you the chance, helping the team shine will get you noticed. It may not be as fast but people will know at the end of the day who did the work and who just took credit for it. Patience is truly a virtue here but karma is on your side. There is a saying about this: "When you shine for others, you cannot help but cast some light on yourself as well." Being noticed and standing out doesn't require that you always be in the spotlight.

Q I appreciate all of your helpful advice on having better meetings in the office, but I find there are too many people in the office who just "put hours in." They don't really care about the success of the company and just want to make a paycheque. How do I deal with colleagues who are completely unmotivated in the workplace?

A Motivation is a huge subject, and what I've always believed is that nobody wakes up in the morning and says to themselves: "Today I am going to be completely unmotivated and will not do a good job." I believe everyone wants to be recognized for their contributions and valued for the work they do. Sometimes, underlying issues make them seem like they are "just there for a paycheque." My recommendation is to find out what they would like to be involved in and find a way for them to get involved. You may be surprised how something very small can trigger a whole new attitude. The key is to take the time to listen and get to know the other individual – beyond the person staring at you across the table at the meeting.

Q It sounds as though planning a meeting in advance is very important. When sending information to participants, how far in advance should I be sure to email everything? Sometimes people send me information five minutes before!

A Setting expectations before a meeting is one of the best ways to make sure you have a productive meeting – that is, one that moves forward. Your email message should clearly state what you need to achieve as a group. If attachments are required pre-reading, make sure you let people know what they should read before the meeting.

People are busy but will read attachments if you ask them to. Don't assume they will open it and read it just because you've attached it.

Ask them to review it and if there is an area that requires special attention, let them know.

As for how far in advance to send? From my experience, a minimum of 24 hours before the meeting is needed. Sending something just prior to the meeting will almost guarantee they will not read it. And if they did, it was only at a cursory level, which means you'll still need to walk them through it.

The purpose of attachments is to make the meeting more efficient. So always keep that in mind when considering how much to send (how much can one absorb prior to a meeting) and how much lead time you give them.

Q I know conference calls are tricky things. You speak of trying to make everyone feel like they're in the same room. Do you have any advice when the technology fails, such as the Internet connection is poor when we're using FaceTime or Skype? Or when a phone line is breaking up and they're not audible?

A Technology is great when it works and a real nuisance when it breaks down. First rule: simply let people know you are having technical issues and to be patient as you work through it. Sometimes it's just a glitch and things snap back to normal. If the technology issue is from someone else and you cannot hear them, simply ask them to hang up and dial back in; sometimes a line can be bad. The objective is to take control of the situation and not get flustered when things go wrong. Everyone has had technology fail on them so it's OK if it happens to you. How you manage through it also says a lot about your ability to lead and solve.

One other thing when you are dealing with technology: have a back-up plan. If everything has truly failed on you, send the group an email to let them know you are working on it and to dial back in 10 minutes. Take control, stay calm and aim to solve, not unravel.

Q I really like the tips for getting people engaged. In my company, meetings have been run the same way for decades, and they're not productive or interesting. As a person with great ideas but not a lot of seniority, what can I do to improve meetings without stepping on toes?

A I would begin with small steps. Bring treats to the meeting – and not just a pack of gum to share. Start with candies or cookies. I personally like popcorn, probably because I associate it with something enjoyable like watching a movie. What you bring is up to you but bring something easy to share.

I would also try using a whiteboard and if there isn't one, a flip chart. It's amazing how people respond to different types of visuals. Get them involved in using these as well. You'd be surprised at how small steps like these can energize a discussion – no aerobics needed!

Q I'm an introvert and find it very difficult to even voice my opinions in a meeting, let alone lead one. Do you have advice for introverts who want to shine?

A Believe it or not, I was very shy when I first started my career. I was always the youngest in the room. I learned to listen very well and not try to say something just to "say something." I would listen to everyone and then based on what I heard, I would ask a question for clarification. People found my questions were helpful and they saw me as someone who was objective. I used this technique for some time and before I knew it, I was speaking a lot more than I ever did. Don't feel you have to compete for air space. Listening well is a lost art so hone that skill. In listening, we learn and as we learn, we grow. Your time to shine is just around the corner.

Q How do you know when it's appropriate to have a face-to-face meeting or a conference call? When will a conference call suffice and when won't it?

A I don't believe there are hard and fast rules about when it's best for a face-to-face or conference call. However, I have always done a face-to-face meeting when these situations present themselves:

• When I need to meet the other individual and learn more about them

• When I have materials I need to show

• When I have to demonstrate something and get a reaction

• When I have to make a strong impression (sales)

For all other situations, it's truly a matter of how well you organize the agenda and objectives, because both mediums are effective.

Q Is there a difference between conference calls and regular face-to-face meetings when it comes to duration? Is it better to make conference calls shorter, since it's harder to gauge the level of attention, or is this something not to worry about when planning a conference call?

A I have had conference calls shorter than face-to-face meetings and ones that are longer. It depends on the agenda and objective. If the intent is to get updates and status reporting, most likely the call will be shorter. However, if it's to get feedback, opinions, or the pros and cons on issues, a conference call will take as long as a regular face-to-face meeting.

The key here is to focus on two things:

• Respect the time of others

• What's on the agenda

Ask yourself what you want to achieve at the end of the call, and let this dictate your time.

Q Is it worth the trouble to use video rather than just voice for conference calls?

A A visual component can help any discussion but it's not what makes a good discussion by itself. Video may enhance the participants' experience, but often the video is set in a place where you cannot see everyone or if you do, they look very far away. Here are some situations where video conferencing will enhance the experience:

- Meeting people you do not know and have not seen before

- Interviewing someone where you want to observe the nonverbal cues

- Seeing visuals, props and physical items that help communicate the story

If the meeting is simply to converse, share or come to an agreement, I believe a voice call is sufficient and less distracting.

Q I work in the IT department and when I hold team meetings, for the life of me, I cannot get anyone talking. I have tried the Play-Doh, markers, food and music. These people are just too shy to say anything when I try to engage them in a discussion. Any advice for how to get a bunch of non-talkers talking?

A   You may be trying a little too hard to get them to speak and engage. I would suggest you ask them what they would like to talk about at the meeting and have them take turns coming up with an agenda. Based on the agenda and who offered the topic for discussion, ask them to lead the discussion. Sometimes it's all about making people accountable at meetings that will get them out of their shell. This is a good development opportunity for them, because one day they, too, will need to hold meetings with their people. Set them up to succeed. Thank them for their contributions in your minutes.

✔ My Action Steps to Brighter Meetings

The next time I have a meeting:

I will start my meetings with objectives such as:

_____ (Page 22)

I will make an effort to "share the chair" with:

_____ (Page 30)

I will stay on track and on time by remembering to:

_____ (Page 33)

I will use this engagement technique:

_____ (Page 38)

I will help people feel as though they are in the room during conference

calls by:

_____ (Page 48)

My Notes:

Did you know?

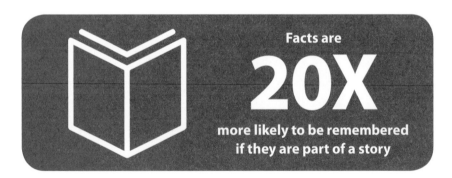

Brighter Presentations

> *"There are always three speeches for every one you actually gave: the one you practised, the one you gave, and the one you wish you gave."*
>
> — Dale Carnegie, American writer and lecturer on self-improvement

Brighter Presentations:
Shine in Front of Others

Have you ever seen a presenter and wished you could deliver with as much ease and confidence?

Have you ever prepared for a presentation only to feel completely unprepared as soon as all eyes turned to you?

Have you ever wondered if there was a secret method to make every presentation a "home run"?

I have a love-hate relationship with presentations. I have been presenting in front of an audience for as long as I've been working. My first presentation was to 23 people at a homebuyers' seminar back in 1990. The group may as well have been 230,000 people because I can still remember how nervous I was as we approached that day. Since then, though, while I still get nervous before any presentation (I really do), I've learned how to control that nervous energy and use it to my advantage. How do I do that? It's not a secret. It's all about deconstruction.

I am a big "deconstructor." By that I mean I always try to break things down into smaller, more manageable parts. You might say I bite-size the fear factor out of presentations. I've learned a long time ago that when we are overwhelmed in life, it's not so much that we're paralyzed by not knowing what to do, but about where to begin. First steps are difficult but once we are in motion, we tend to stay in motion and the rest becomes easier.

How I approach the fear or paralysis of preparing for and delivering presentations is to break things down. What are the key hurdles for any presentation that we need to get our heads around?

- Managing fear: What if I choke?

- Relevant content: What if they hate my content?

- Audience engagement: What if they completely zone out?

- Energy in delivery: What if I don't come across well?

By deconstructing presentations into these smaller, more manageable components, you can deal with each one of them directly and not be overwhelmed. Each one of these hurdles can be overcome with practice, honest reflection and insights I will share with you, along with some of my best learning experiences.

Let's begin with fear.

Brighter Presentations: *Know What's Within Your Control and What is Not*

"What would you do if you weren't afraid?"

You're standing to the side of the stage, waiting to be introduced while the previous speaker basks in applause. You fear you won't be as funny or engaging or even as informative as she was. The host is now introducing you. Twenty seconds before your name is called, panic sets in. The audience has just been told you're an expert who's going to share great insights. Looking at the crowd, all you feel is fear – constricted throat, pounding heart, sweaty palms and wobbly knees.

But it doesn't have to be this way!

Think about the last time you told a friend about a great movie you'd just seen, an amazing event you attended or a fabulous restaurant experience you had. Were you nervous speaking to them? Absolutely not. Why would you be? After all, it was an experience or topic you were very familiar with. Your excitement would have come through, you were probably quite animated as you shared your story, and it felt like time just flew by as you recounted your story. It was easy, enjoyable and entertaining to your listener.

Now imagine I asked you to recount the very same experience, but instead of telling the person next to you, you had to present it in front of the room full of people – many of whom you do not know. If you're like most people, the ease, enjoyment and entertaining factor would most likely diminish, or worse, you may even become anxious, somewhat robotic and awkward as you shared your experience. You likely would leave out all the emotions, facial expressions and non-verbal gestures you would have made when you told this to your friend. Why is that? It's the same story or recounting of an experience. What made the difference?

Where does this anxiety come from? What is the one thing we're most fearful of when it comes to presenting? What are we afraid of?

There are many reasons why you would become anxious in front of people: Making mistakes, not sounding like an expert or realizing there are other experts in the room who may know more than you, or getting a question you cannot answer.

In my experience and having seen, heard and spoken with many who present on a regular basis, the root cause of anxiety is the fear of being judged. We're concerned they will not like us, what we're saying is inaccurate or wrong, or perhaps we're not experienced enough to speak on this topic. When we feel like we're being judged, we tend to focus all our attention on those who are giving us those signals, such as frowns, crossed arms or perplexed facial expressions. It's tough when you're faced with someone who is frowning at you, because you're wondering if you're getting through. The result is that you end up focusing on that individual because you want to win them over. In fact, you're so focused on winning them over that you forget about all the other people in the room.

The other challenge with trying to win over this individual by putting all your energy in his or her direction is that you may have interpreted the signal incorrectly. They may be frowning because they are trying to read what you have on the screen or that that may be their natural facial expression. They may have their arms crossed because again, it's their natural state or the room is chilly. Whether these signals indicate you're being judged or otherwise, it is something you cannot control. You cannot control *what* people are thinking. If they think you're too young, too inexperienced or not credible or even that they don't like you, you can do very little to change what they *think*. This is what I mean by don't try to control what you cannot. Instead, focus on controlling what you can.

Four Things You Can Control

1. Your planning

2. Your tone and pace

3. Your words

4. Your enthusiasm

1. Your Planning

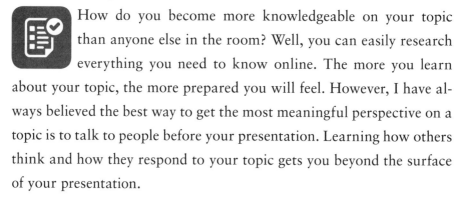 How do you become more knowledgeable on your topic than anyone else in the room? Well, you can easily research everything you need to know online. The more you learn about your topic, the more prepared you will feel. However, I have always believed the best way to get the most meaningful perspective on a topic is to talk to people before your presentation. Learning how others think and how they respond to your topic gets you beyond the surface of your presentation.

People love to know what others think. After all, some of the most revealing research is based on interviews and focus groups. Research increases the credibility of information. That is a fact. How others see and experience a product, solution, service or offering gives you an invaluable amount of insight that others will find interesting, engaging and memorable. So the next time you are preparing for a presentation – on any topic – plan to talk with others, learn their opinions and get their likes and dislikes. I assure you your content will have greater depth and richness. Invest time in becoming a true subject matter expert. People will notice and value your work.

2. Your Tone and Pace

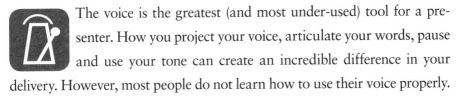 The voice is the greatest (and most under-used) tool for a presenter. How you project your voice, articulate your words, pause and use your tone can create an incredible difference in your delivery. However, most people do not learn how to use their voice properly.

It's important to first remember that warming up your voice and relaxing your neck is not only for singers. Take the time to try this!

Next, envision tone and pace as your "highlighters" to your audience. Just like what a highlighter does for the reader – bring out important points you want to emphasize or remember – your tone and pace have the same effect for your audience.

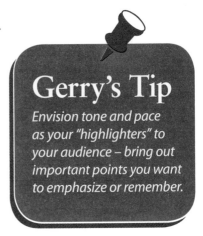

Gerry's Tip

Envision tone and pace as your "highlighters" to your audience – bring out important points you want to emphasize or remember.

Everyone gets nervous when they speak in front of people, even me! No matter how many times I stand in front of a large audience (not that I've counted but I imagine it is well over 1,000 times in the past 10 years), I still have nerves at the beginning of the presentation. And when we're nervous, we tend to speak very quickly. I'm sure you have witnessed this in others as well. It's as though we just want to get through it, like a race to the final points.

So here's the first thing to do with regard to your pace: S-L-O-W I-T D-O-W-N for the first five minutes, as you get your groove and feel for your environment – whether it's on stage, in front of the room or at the lectern (although I hope you'll avoid standing behind the lectern).

Here are four ways to help slow things down and get you to feel the groove as you deliver your content. Use the first five minutes to:

- Greet the audience. Ask them how they are. How was traffic getting here? How was lunch/dinner? Depending on your audience, I am sure you can find a few (not just one) questions to get them engaged with you. You will feel much less "alone on stage" when you do this.

- Tell them a little about yourself. No notes here, please. You should know who you are at all times.

- Relate to the previous speakers' content or to the overall event theme, to help tie things together.

- Tell a story that relates the presentation you're about to give to the event they are attending. Stories are a great way to connect with the audience and people love to get to know the "personal side" of any presenter because it gives them an idea of *who* you are. People are naturally curious.

After you have taken the first five minutes to breathe and get comfortable with your environment, you are ready to get into your presentation.

Let's now talk about tone. How many times have you heard someone say: "They were so monotone and it put me to sleep when they spoke"? Being monotone is the worst way to speak. No one speaks naturally in a monotone voice but when we are nervous, the robotic nature can take over and suddenly we sound like the voice from an old GPS or worse yet, the computer H.A.L from *2001: A Space Odyssey.*

It's hard to describe tone but you know it when you hear it. We've all experienced when someone's comments have a particular tone – perhaps a harshness – that is perceived as negative. However, we can use tone in a very positive way when we are presenting.

Tone can be described as seeing your voice go up and down like a roller coaster. It's a melodic approach to speaking because tone, like a high-lighter, is about emphasis. Where you place the emphasis creates tone.

Exercise
Read this sentence aloud and try to convey different emotions using the same words spoken with different tones: **"I really like your new hairstyle."**

By emphasizing the word *really,* you can create either a tone of sincerity or sarcasm.

By emphasizing the word *like,* you can create a genuine feel.

By emphasizing *I,* you can let the individual know that *only you* like her new hairstyle.

By emphasizing *new,* you could convey the idea that you didn't like the previous style.

Tone is about emphasis, and your ability to apply this to your delivery will add depth and colour to what you are saying. Again, this is something totally within your control.

How to get rid of your **H.UM.P**

Another enemy of presenters is the dreaded "Ums." You can identify this only if you listen to a recording of yourself, which I highly recommend for those just starting to do presentations. "Ums" occur when our talking speed is faster than the speed at which the brain can give us the next set of words to deliver. Knowing you have the "Um problem" is a big step in fixing it. Yes, it can be fixed if you work at it. I used to have an "Um" problem so I am speaking, um, from experience.

I fixed my H.UM.P (Huge UM Problem) by learning how to embrace the idea of a pause. Pausing is natural, just like breathing, but for some reason, we are afraid of the pause. Lesson one: do not be afraid of the pause. Lesson two: the pause is your friend!

> ### Gerry's Tip
> Ums occur when our talking speed is faster than the recall speed from our brain. Knowing you have the "Um problem" is a big step in fixing it.

"It's not so much knowing when to speak, but knowing when to pause."

— Jack Benny, American actor and comedian

When you slow down your pace of speech and learn how to effectively pause, it *will* become your natural state of speaking. Here are some tips on how to apply your new friend, the pause:

- If you are delivering a speech (something written that has to be said word for word), like an announcement, a tribute, an introduction, etc., simply put in brackets the word "PAUSE" where it's appropriate.

- If you are delivering a presentation where slides are used, use each animation of your bullets to remind you of the need to pause.

- Use trigger words to help you remember what you're talking about next. A trigger word helps you immediately know what to say next. Note that I say trigger *word*(s), not sentences. The trick is to be able to look down at your notes and quickly grab these trigger words and focus back on your audience.

Remember that H.UM.P happens when your brain is not getting you the words quickly enough, so the above tips are ways to help make the connection between brain and mouth just a little smoother.

Getting over the H.UM.P takes practice, but the most important thing is to *not* be afraid to pause. Pausing has another great effect, other than relieving you of the H.UM.P It makes the audience pay more attention to what you are about to say next. Notice the next time you pause in between or midway through a sentence. Your audience will be silent and wait for what you're about to say next. This is a very effective way to get an important point across.

3. Your Words

So far, we've covered two things completely within your control: your planning as well as your tone and pace. The third is your words. I know so many people who write out what they want to say, rehearse it in their heads and then expect their delivery to be flawless. I can tell you that if you rehearse only in your head, you will not have a convincing delivery. The problem with this is something called *writing for the eyes vs. writing for the ears.* This is a common mistake of presenters who do more writing than speaking. When we write for the eyes, the structure of the sentence is critical. The specific words chosen, the phrasing and the punctuation make a convincing sentence or paragraph. However, when we speak, the audience is listening with their ears, not their eyes. Sounds too obvious? Perhaps, but I have heard many people give presentations and speeches that fail to connect with the audience for this exact reason. They may as well have read a brochure to me.

> **Gerry's Tip**
>
> Don't be afraid to pause during your presentation. It will slow down your thoughts and get the audience to pay more attention to what you are about to say next.

"If you can't explain it to a six year old, you don't understand it yourself."

— Albert Einstein, German-born theoretical physicist

Perfect words that look great on paper, say in a booklet or advertisement, are not what the audience wants. They want simple, easy-to-understand language. I will talk more about this in the following chapters on the different types of presentations and how best to deliver your content. But for now, deliver your presentation out loud. And, yes, standing in front of a mirror helps. Or practice with someone who will be a good critic and not someone who will just say "That sounds great"! And if they do say that, ask them why it sounds great, and what three things they remember about what you just said. If they cannot do that – it wasn't that "great." Sorry.

4. Your Enthusiasm

Here's another area you can totally control: your excitement in speaking with others. I often have a little chuckle to myself when I hear presenters say they are excited about being there, but it really sounds like "Oh, I really wish I didn't have to do this!" Now don't get me wrong, being excited or enthusiastic is not about how loud you are or how high you are bouncing. Those are two ways of expressing it, but that's not what I am referring to.

Enthusiasm can come only from inside your heart. Not your mind. How you demonstrate this enthusiasm is a combination of simultaneous actions:

- *Your smile*

- *Your eyes*

- *Your posture*

These non-verbal gestures, working in concert, tell the audience you're happy to be there and are truly excited about telling them something worth listening to. But first you have to believe this. If you don't personally believe the message you are about to share, no one will believe you. *You must be believed to be heard.*

Everyone has a different energy level when they present. Some are naturally higher than others, and that's OK. No one should "act" like someone else. Effective presenters know their style is their own; they don't try to mimic someone else's. As the quote often attributed to Oscar Wilde says:

"Be yourself. Everyone else is already taken."

A final reminder. Control what you can – and there's lots you can control from what I have just shared with you. Forget about trying to control what you cannot. Let that go. Once you let go, you will be able to free yourself from the added stress of presenting and begin finding your own style; that is, who you are as a presenter. Next, incorporate these lessons as you build your own brand. To reiterate: People want to listen to *you*, not the you trying to sound like someone else.

My story of letting go of what I cannot control

In 1998, I was working at one of Canada's top financial institutions in the corporate training area. We were doing satellite training, which meant we broadcast from the Toronto studio across the country to all the branches in Canada. Each branch had a little satellite dish, so they would turn on the TV and suddenly see this information. Management suggested that since I was in corporate training, I should be on camera. They sent me to a media coach and I remember how fearful I was in front of the camera. Having to deliver in front of people was already difficult, but manageable. In front of a camera was a whole new experience. More than the awkwardness of talking into the lens of a camera, I had another very real fear. I have a glass eye and I did not want the viewing audience to see my eyes move around differently. I had a fear of looking like the English character actor Marty Feldman, whose big eyes seemed to move in different directions.

The advice from the media coach was this: "This is something you can't control, but what you can control is how your excitement about this new initiative comes across on camera. And that's what people will see. If you worry about your eye doing something weird, that's all you're going to focus on."

I ended up joining a team of presenters who were dedicated to presenting on camera to audiences across the country. I learned about what I could control and honed those skills well. As time passed, I was able to distinguish – on and off camera, in work and in my personal life – what was within my control and what was not. It's a powerful feeling of freedom to let go. I am continuing to learn this today.

Content and Audience Engagement

We've all been to presentations where the presenter changed the title slide, did a "search and replace" of key words and *voilà*, their presentation was ready! Adding your company's logo and inserting a line from your CEO does not make it customized and your audience knows it. Content – and more importantly – relevant content is what your audience will connect with. It's what makes them nod in agreement when you are presenting. Don't you love seeing that? I do!

So how do we avoid the "one-size-fits-all" trap and begin delivering content that is customized? A great presentation is all about *"How can I help you?"* Always start with that objective.

Gerry's Tip

A great presentation is all about "How can I help you?" Always start with that objective.

How can I help you?

- Become better at what you do
- Be more informed and aware
- Get faster at getting things done
- Act more competitively than others
- Be more efficient at what you do
- Achieve your goals

Identifying how you can help your audience will not only customize the presentation you're about to make, but will also make it extremely relevant – and that's a powerful presentation!

The Four Types of Presentations

Once you have figured out how you can help them, next determine which of the four types of presentations will be most effective at helping them:

1. **Educational – skills and knowledge enhancement**

2. **Entertaining – elevate moods and sense of occasion**

3. **Informational – awareness building**

4. **Motivational – move them to action**

It's important to know that while your presentation can fall into one of the four categories, it is also quite possible and interesting to audiences to have components of all four types of presentations in your session. Let's look at each type a little closer and how you can engage the audience during these presentations.

1. Educational

If your presentation needs to educate your audience and enhance their skills and knowledge, here are five interesting ways to customize and engage to create a brighter presentation:

- *Be clear about your objectives* – Communicate upfront what you hope they will learn. What will they improve after this session? What's the advantage for them to pay attention? What's in it for them?

- *Move from the familiar to the unfamiliar* – If you are introducing a new model or process, try to start with something they already know and do well. Begin with a model or process they are familiar with, and then show the enhancements being made in the new version. It is always easier to move from an area of familiarity than to try to introduce something brand new at the top of your presentation. References to the past are a great way to move people to the future.

- *Use analogies* – If you are trying to explain a problem or issue that needs a solution, try using an analogy to bring the point home. Sometimes, taking your audience to a place where there is universal understanding of a problem or issue will help them gain insight into their own problem or issue. An example of this would be if you are trying to improve service levels within your organization. Rather than start with their specific situation, begin with something they all can relate to, such as service at a restaurant, hotel or other familiar setting. Taking them outside their work environment makes it less contentious and opens up discussion more easily and with less risk.

- *Practise* – People learn by doing, not listening. If you are showing them a new approach, technique or process, have them try it themselves. The ability to work through the new skills and knowledge is essential for learning to transfer. I have always found case studies and simulations to be the most effective in helping audiences learn and discover for themselves areas of strengths and weaknesses. When your audience can see for themselves, rather than you telling them, they gain a much better understanding of the new skill and increase the likelihood they will take it away with them.

- *Test them, but make it fun* – People are competitive by nature. Make it entertaining by turning it into a contest, and you'll see how much more people learn and remember what your presentation was about.

2. Entertaining

 This type of presentation ranges from a keynote to emceeing an event, when your presentation needs to entertain your audience and elevate their mood and sense of occasion. Here are four interesting ways to engage your audience to create a brighter presentation:

- *Share Stories* – Using stories is a powerful way to touch an audience's heart and mind. Stories – whether from personal experience, an experience of something you have witnessed or even a fictional story – are an efficient way to lead audiences into your presentation. Personally, I've found that presenters who share something from their own experience help me relate to them and what the larger event is about.

- *Play Music* – Music is perhaps one of the best mood enhancers. You don't need to look too far to see how music elevates audiences and creates a true sense of occasion. Finding the right music takes time and patience. Here are some guidelines to use when trying to find the song that will create the right mood:

  - The music needs to be recognizable by many, if not all. It may be your new favourite song, but if no one knows it, it will not elevate the room.

  - It should carry a message that aligns to the event.

- Lyrics should not be offensive. People do pay attention to the words.

- If you use commercial music, check with your audio/visual provider to ensure you comply with copyright rules in your jurisdiction.

- *Involve People* – Audience involvement is important in any presentation, but especially in a presentation that needs to entertain and elevate the mood. Audiences need to feel special, be the centre of attention, and to know why your event is "an occasion." Be clear about the occasion and if it's a celebration, celebrate. If it's to recognize individuals, make them feel they are the most important people in the room. Remember the Oscar ceremony in 2014, where emcee Ellen DeGeneres took the show right into the audience in the theatre. Her ability to engage with them made that entire show different. While I am not proposing that you always go out to your audience to involve them, it is worth thinking about what is the best way to draw them in and how best to use their energy to elevate the mood in the room.

- *Offer Games* – I have successfully used games to get audiences to have some fun. Again, when the occasion is meant to be fun, people are ready to have some fun. Games I have used range from simple ones like trivia or "Name That Song" to more complicated ones that resemble real game shows such as *Don't Forget the Lyrics*, *Family Feud* and *Deal or No Deal*. The actual game is not the most important thing. Having something that is easy, fun and competitive is a great way to create a true sense of occasion for everyone.

3. Informational

 If your presentation needs to inform your audience and build awareness, here are five techniques to engage your audience to create a brighter presentation:

Gerry's Tip

People remember things in threes and fours. Any more than that, it becomes overwhelming to retain.

- *Did you Know?* – Facts and figures are a powerful way to get a point across to your audience. Use them throughout your presentation to set up a topic or section. The more visual you make the stats, the more memorable it will be.

- *Threes and Fours* – People remember things in threes and fours. Any more than that, it becomes too hard to remember. Take each section of your presentation and keep it to no more than four key messages. Some of the best presentations I've attended are where speakers say: "I just want you to remember these three things." And people will remember them!

- *Trivia* – Trivia is the reverse of showing your audience stats and figures. Instead, ask them. Using trivia in the form of true/false or multiple choice will help them remember and create more engagement than just telling them. You might even try to get the audience to vote by raising their hands (e.g., "How many of you have ever ..."). This is a great way to engage your audience throughout the presentation.

- *Testimonials* – Statements and testimonials serve as validation to any points you are making. People like to know that others feel or think the same way. Credibility is increased when others support what you are saying.

- *Video* – Inserting video clips into your presentation is another nice way to engage your audience as well as bring your points across in a different way. Video clips provide a voice other than yours and allow presenters to take a brief break to gather their thoughts for the next segment. Inserting video clips is no longer expensive, nor does it require an entire cast and crew, thanks to modern technology. Just take a look at YouTube to find a short clip to insert into your presentation. Some guidelines for inserting clips:

  - Keep it short – on average, less than three minutes.

  - Make sure it's relevant and not just a battery of information thrown at your audience.

  - If it's funny, make sure it's not offensive.

  - Always debrief the clip and tie it back to your presentation or a key point that the clip supports.

  - Explain to your audience why you chose this particular clip.

4. Motivational

 If your presentation needs to motivate your audience and move them to action, here are six interesting ways to engage your audience and create a brighter presentation:

- *Facts and Stats* – One powerful statistic can be more memorable than a series of bullet points. Always remember your audience has only a limited capacity to retain information. Use their brain real estate wisely.

- *Visuals for Impact* – You've heard the saying that a picture is worth a thousand words. You don't need to look much farther than Facebook entries to see how pictures, images and cartoons can say so much. Leverage the use of visuals where you can to make your statement.

Gerry's Tip

Video clips provide a voice other than yours and allow the presenter to take a brief break to gather his or her thoughts for the next segment.

- *Compelling Win* – Everyone likes to gain something or to not lose something they already have. Pain and gain are great motivators for people to move to action. Find out what your audience's win is and show them how to get there.

- *Easy Steps* - We like simple and easy. If you make the win too complicated or it has more steps than the Great Wall of China, people will not even take one single step. Make it easy for your audience. Think about how many times you have seen smart advertisers use the term "in three easy steps."

- *Personal Commitments to Change* – Asking your audience to do something at the end of your presentation is a good thing. Sometimes, we know what we "should" do but if no one asks us to do it, we can take a passive approach to change. Invite them to be part of the change. Give them permission, ask for support or encourage them to challenge themselves – all of which will help motivate them to action.

- *Support* – Once you have compelled them to change, make sure you have a method to help them through the change. When people start taking steps or move in the direction you have asked of them, provide support by way of information, people or other resources to show they are not doing this alone.

Developing content with a "How can I help you?" focus and applying the various techniques I've shared with you will engage and energize your audience. Let's now talk a little more about where energy comes from.

Delivering with Energy and Authenticity

"**Where do you get your energy from when you present?** I want some of that energy!"

I cannot tell you how many times I have been asked this question after I present. One-third of my energy comes from knowing I've prepared well, which means I'm excited to share what I have created. I'm still nervous, but I am prepared and ready.

Another third of my energy comes from being nervous. The ability to use the nervous energy, instead of being crippled by it, is something I hope to share with you.

The final third of my energy comes from my Grade 13 theatre class. Being "on" for me is turning on a mental switch in my head when I know I have to bring my A-game to the table. Like an actor who gets into character, I get into my "show time" persona. It's still me, but with all the other distractions removed. I am focused and in my perfect zone for this presentation.

These past sections talked about how to plan and prepare for a presentation that is engaging, fun, useful, relevant and memorable. I call that the "physical" aspect of preparation. What I will now share with you are my "mental" (game-on) preparation strategies.

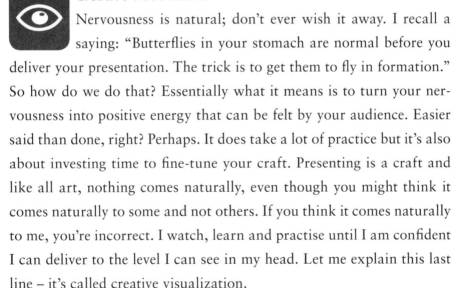 Creative Visualization

Nervousness is natural; don't ever wish it away. I recall a saying: "Butterflies in your stomach are normal before you deliver your presentation. The trick is to get them to fly in formation." So how do we do that? Essentially what it means is to turn your nervousness into positive energy that can be felt by your audience. Easier said than done, right? Perhaps. It does take a lot of practice but it's also about investing time to fine-tune your craft. Presenting is a craft and like all art, nothing comes naturally, even though you might think it comes naturally to some and not others. If you think it comes naturally to me, you're incorrect. I watch, learn and practise until I am confident I can deliver to the level I can see in my head. Let me explain this last line – it's called creative visualization.

Seeing yourself successful in preparing for your presentation is as important as (if not more than) rehearsing your points or creating your presentation deck. Seeing myself successfully deliver a presentation is how I turn my nervousness into positive energy. I already know what the perfect outcome is in my head, so all I need to do is to match that image with what I am about to do. For me, it's kind of like painting by numbers. The instructions for creating a beautiful painting are already there. I just need to follow them.

I wish this was my idea but it's not. Many authors have written about this, including one of my favourites, Stephen Covey, who, in *Seven Habits of Highly Effective People* named an entire chapter after this: "Begin with the end in mind."

What I do is completely walk through the entire presentation, but not only the part when I'm in front of the audience. I start visualizing well before that. Perhaps the best way to explain this is to walk you through the 24 hours before I present and take you on a journey inside my head. (Well, not my entire head ☺.)

Countdown to Presentation: 24 Hours 24:00

 All my notes are ready, whether they are PowerPoint slides or pages of a script to read.

 I review my notes. Usually they are on index cards because I like to walk around on stage.

 I use a Sharpie marker to underline trigger words or words of importance that I will make sure I use.

I write out word for word (for rehearsal only) what I open with and close with. The take-off and landing of your presentation needs flawless execution, like a plane.

 Once I am clear on exactly what I want to say in my opening and closing, I transfer the words to index cards as well. Writing out your opening and closing cannot be understated. Take time to do this. Skipping it will guarantee the H.UM.P.s in your first five minutes – what I deem the most nervous part. Why put yourself through that?

 Now I have all my index cards, with underlined or circled key words along with a methodical opening and closing.

Countdown to Presentation: 12 Hours 12:00

 I visualize I am at the event/conference/meeting.

 I see familiar faces and I see myself mingling with people. It's a safe environment and I am comfortable and relaxed in my visualization.

You can take this further – and I have in the past – by using all your senses when you visualize. Smell the coffee and imagine pastries on the table. How do they taste? These details help the visualization seem real.

Here are some things (and don't limit yourself here) you can visualize to create a safe environment:

- The room

- The furniture

- Table or venue (if you know what the room looks like)

- You talking with others and smiling or laughing

- Others responding to your energy

- The smell of coffee, breakfast or even flowers

- You shaking hands, perhaps with your boss or others with whom you would normally shake hands

- You being comfortable and enjoying the interaction with others

 I continue with this visualization but now I see myself waiting to be introduced.

Here are some things I visualize:

- I see myself sitting at the table with some of my colleagues around me.

- I see myself reviewing the index cards with my opening remarks – thinking through my first few lines of the opening.

- I feel good and I can see I have a relaxed look on my face. I am smiling or maybe even laughing at a joke the person on stage is telling.

Again, in my visualization, I am relaxed, happy to be there and ready for my presentation.

 I now visualize me being introduced and walking on stage.

Here are some things I visualize:

- I see myself ready with my index cards

- When I am introduced, I see people looking at me and smiling; I am smiling back.

- I feel ready. My name is called.

- I see myself walk to the stage but I am not looking at my feet or hurrying.

- I am looking at the person who introduced me and walking with confidence, and I am smiling.

- I see myself shaking hands with the individual who introduced me and I hear myself saying "thank you" to him.

- I see myself glancing at the screen and see my presentation is there. I also see the remote clicker to advance the slides right there in front of me and I approach it.

- I look at the audience. I smile and take my time before I utter one word.

- After I see myself scan the audience smiling back at me, I see myself saying how great it is to be there.

I'm now on stage and have started to speak. My visualization continues as I deliver my presentation.

Here are some things I visualize:

IMPORTANT: While you're visualizing, if you see yourself doing something incorrectly or you mess up the opening words in your head– simply restart where you left off. Remember, this is your movie in your head and you're the director and producer and star!

- I hear my opening word for word.

- I hear my opening lines. As I visualize, they are perfect and I can hear myself speaking more slowly than I usually do. This is on purpose since I realize that in the first five minutes, I tend to speed up my rate of speech.

- I see myself nailing the opening and begin engaging the audience by either asking them a question or asking them to raise their hands in a vote.

- I see them participating in my voting question and I use their response to lead into my presentation.

- My visualization continues but at this stage I do not need to visualize every word or aspect of the presentation.

- Remember that for most presenters, the challenge is the first five to 10 minutes of the presentation, and now that I have visualized the success of these first few minutes in my head, I have set what the success image looks like.

IMPORTANT: I now have a reference point of what success and energy looks like for me. This mental programming is not only good from a preparation perspective, but it also actually helps train your brain into thinking you have done this before – and it is in fact this training of the brain that simulates actually doing it.

 I continue with this visualization but now I visualize myself closing the presentation.

Here are some things I visualize:

- I see myself reaching the final few slides.

- I see questions being asked, people raising their hands and me answering with them nodding in understanding and appreciation.

- I see them smiling and I feel confident I have provided them with what they needed.

- I see my final slide and recite my closing remarks. Every word I hear are the words in my written closing. I hear myself nailing the closing.

- I see myself thanking the audience for their participation and the opportunity to share useful information with them.

- I see them applaud me. In fact, I hear them applaud me – and it's loud.

- They are smiling and so am I.

- What a fantastic presentation I just gave!

IMPORTANT: Your brain has been trained! Congratulations!

You have one shot to deliver your presentation. But when you visualize your perfect presentation, you have as many times, as many takes and as many repeats as you would like. Don't underestimate the power of visualization. Not only do I do this, but world athletes have also been doing this for years to create successes in their minds.

Visualizing yourself successful is one of the most important pieces of advice I can share to help you make your presentations a whole lot brighter.

Last words: Practise, practise, practise – as though you were right there, right now, and your audience is in front of you.

A Flashback From Gerry

I still remember my early days as a presenter. As a learning specialist, I delivered an average of five workshops a month, plus presentations, conference hosting and keynote addresses. Before each event began, I felt as though I was going to be sick. I was anxious, nervous and definitely not myself. I used to go into the bathroom and sit inside the stall (and yes, at times suffer the dry heaves) just to pull myself together. That was my reality for a long time until I realized that feeling nervous, anxious and almost being sick could actually work in my favour.

It occurred to me that what I was feeling – though very uncomfortably real – was in fact a form of energy, adrenaline if you will. And what I realized was that energy is energy – it's all how you choose to use it. Yes, I was nervous; but instead of interpreting this nervousness as being unprepared (which I was not), I saw my nervousness as "all systems ready to blast off." I began to envision the inside of my body as a series of panels of light bulbs, and as I got closer to my time to present, these panels of lights were being turned on one panel at a time and when all the panels were on – I was ready to "bring it on"!

Later in my career, I saw this as "being in the zone" – not a zone of nervousness or anxiety, but a zone of readiness and anticipation of something that was going to be great. Later on in this book, you'll see that for me, how I think and interpret what's happening around me has a significant impact on outcomes in my career and in my life.

Remember, nervous energy is still energy. It's all in how you choose to see it and use it.

 Lecterns

"Make sure you have finished speaking before your audience has finished listening."

— Dorothy Sarnoff, American opera singer, actor and self-help coach

Lecterns definitely serve a purpose and are necessary in some cases, such as large, formal gatherings. Think of churches, political rallies and huge outdoor events.

For me, however, when I am trying to connect with my audience, a lectern is not the way to do it. That being said, I completely understand the comfort of having a solid lectern in front of you. You can place your notes and your water on it, and perhaps even treat it as an anchor to hold onto when you're feeling just a little nervous when you speak.

These are all legitimate reasons why you would want to use a lectern, but they come at a cost. I believe the lectern is a barrier that affects your connection with the audience. When I first started speaking in public, I did often rely on one. Today, when I think of a lectern, in my mind I envision a lion tamer with a whip in one hand and a chair in the other. He is stuck behind a barrier trying to keep me at a distance, as though he is vulnerable.

Being away from the lectern certainly increases the speaker's vulnerability with the audience, but it is also one of the most effective ways to connect with them.

I'm not a particularly political person but I do like watching politicians on stage. In fact, I learn a lot about speaking from studying them. I recall back in 1996 when U.S. vice president Bob Dole was running for president. His wife, Elizabeth Dole, gave a speech on his behalf at one event, and I remember this as clearly as if it happened yesterday. After Ms. Dole was introduced by the host, she walked on stage with much fanfare, music and applause. She strode up to the lectern and did her usual thank yous and mentioned how wonderful a reception she received and how touched she was.

What she did next is what I remember well. She said: "I am here to speak on behalf of Bob but I am also here to speak to you as friends. And as your friend, I wish I could be sitting with you in my living room having this chat. And since I cannot do that, I'd still like to be closer to you. Would that be all right?" The audience cheered to a point of deafening applause. Elizabeth Dole then walked away from the podium, moved on to centre stage and then proceeded to walk down the stairs and stopped just in front of the first row of the audience. She then said: "Now this is better!"

She completed her speech to perhaps the loudest standing ovation I had heard until the days of Barack Obama's campaign. My point here is that she knew exactly what she wanted to do and understood how distance and barriers significantly reduce the connection with the audience. I still think of that speech sometimes when I am on stage and, yes, it has moved me at times to get right into the audience.

Four Steps to Staying Away from the Lectern

I know what you're thinking right now: "How can I possibly do that *and* still remember what I need to say?" This is a very fair point.

My objective is not to have you become like Elizabeth Dole tomorrow. Rather, I recommend that you not use the lectern as a crutch. As I mentioned, I have used lecterns in the past, so now I'd like to help you to *step away* and in the future completely *stay away* from lecterns so you can better connect with your audience.

Step 1: Trust Yourself

Having your notes with you *all* the time will guarantee one thing: you will look at them. It's human nature that when you have something written you will read it and not trust the fact that you do in fact know your material. Aside from reading a formal speech or lengthy introduction, you should not need to rely on every word written in your notes. You know this stuff, so trust yourself and know that the more you do not "read the words" as written, the more you will sound natural and authentic

Step 2: "But I Need My Prompts!"

Fair enough. Prompts are trigger words or images that help you flow into what you wish to share with your audience. In North America and around the globe, PowerPoint is the most relied upon form of visual prompts. And that's OK as long as your slides are prompts and not your entire speech written as bullets. I'm sure you know what I mean. We've all seen this painful way of presenting.

Another very useful prompt employed by professional speakers and interviewers is the cue card. These are the small index cards you can buy at any stationery store. When I use cue cards, I have at my fingertips all the trigger points, quotes, important names and places when I need them.

Step 3: Step Away from the Lectern

This is the most difficult step. Here's how I suggest you do it:

1. Be sure you've prepared your slides and cue cards so they provide easily identifiable prompts for you. That's why they were originally called *visual aids*. The slides are designed to help you with the delivery, but they are not what the audience should be looking at. You and your message should be the focus of the audience.

2. Start at the lectern. Bring your water and, if you must, place your notes or hard copy of your slides there – ideally before you go up on stage if you can.

3. When you're at the lectern, say your thank yous and introductory remarks.

4. Before your fifth slide, begin to step away from the lectern; carry your cue cards, which contain your trigger words aligned with the rest of your slides.

Step 4: Be Comfortable Going Back to the Lectern

Yes, I've said to step away from the lectern, but it's all right to go back to refer to your notes or have a drink of water. The lectern is not the enemy here; the key is to not let it control how you connect with your audience.

A technique I use if I want to get back to the lectern – say for a drink or to take a look at my notes – is to simply ask the audience a question. By asking them a question, for example: "Do you recall a time when this has happened to you? How did it make you feel?" you have a golden opportunity to get back to the lectern and take a sip of water or look over your notes. This is completely OK and very natural to your audience.

Two tips here: Sipping water is a must. When we are nervous, our mouths become drier than normal and when we speak, we tend to make a smacking sound. My experience on camera has taught me this and that's why I always have water with me and am always taking a sip when I find those golden opportunities.

My second tip is to never get water with ice. Not because it's too cold; I like very cold water. It's because ice in a glass makes us dribble. Yes, dribble! It spills slightly while you're drinking, and you have to wipe your mouth. And there's no napkin! Just stick to water *sans* ice and you'll thank me later.

When You *Should* Use a Lectern

To be fair, there are times when a lectern has a place in your presentation. Here are occasions when I believe a lectern is necessary:

An Elevation Issue

 If you are in front of a large audience and they are at a level where they cannot see you properly, a lectern can be helpful.

The Only Microphone is on the Lectern

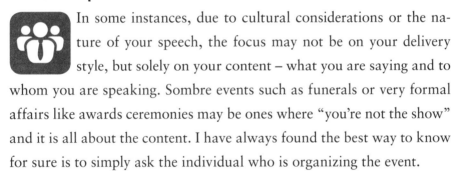 I have been to venues where the only microphone is attached to the lectern. If it is not moveable, you have to stay behind the lectern. However, I have been in situations where the microphone is bendable. In this situation, I angle it so I am able to stand beside (not behind) the lectern to do my presentation. It's always good to know what is available before heading to the venue where you're going to speak. You don't want surprises! If you can, request a lavaliere microphone that you can attach to your clothing.

Audience Expectations

In some instances, due to cultural considerations or the nature of your speech, the focus may not be on your delivery style, but solely on your content – what you are saying and to whom you are speaking. Sombre events such as funerals or very formal affairs like awards ceremonies may be ones where "you're not the show" and it is all about the content. I have always found the best way to know for sure is to simply ask the individual who is organizing the event.

I hope I've been able to convince you to think differently about lecterns and to try a few things to get away from this barrier the next time you present in front of a larger audience. I know this can be very intimidating, but I have seen so many people become amazing presenters just by taking these few steps.

I know you can do this too!

Recap

Key hurdles for shining as a presenter

1. Managing fear

2. Focusing on relevant content

3. Audience engagement

4. Keeping energy in delivery

Four things you *can* control

1. Your planning

2. Your tone and pace

3. Your words

4. Your enthusiasm

Four types of presentations

1. Educational – skills and knowledge enhancement

2. Entertaining – elevate moods and sense of occasion

3. Informational – awareness building

4. Motivational – move them to action

Ask Gerry

Q I liked all of your information on giving "brighter presentations," but I often lose my train of thought when presenting. For some reason I can't help my mind shifting to what people are thinking about me, instead of the content of my presentation! Any advice?

A Look for the friendly face; there is always one in the crowd. I find we tend to slip into the "they-hate-me syndrome" when we see someone who looks uninterested or bored. Instead, focus on someone who is making good eye contact with you. I always find people in the first three rows are more engaged. They choose these seats for a reason – to be closer to what's happening at the front of the room. So look for the friendly faces there and you'll feel like a rock star in no time! (Just don't ignore the rest of the audience.)

Q I often find myself speaking in a presentation similar to how I would speak to a friend one-on-one. I'm not sure this is effective to engage the audience. I'd like to strike a balance between being conversational and approachable and the "performance" aspect of presenting. Any tips?

A There is a difference between speaking as though you are in a one-to-one conversation with your audience and talking to only one member of that audience. The latter makes you focus on this one person or their question so much that you have disengaged others. Creating a sense of informality and showing vulnerability is what makes audiences connect with you. Make sure you are scanning the room and making eye contact with others in the middle and at the back of the room. Sometimes focusing only on the front row can make you feel you have lost the others. Just remember this: you have something to share with this audience. Your enthusiasm and interest in the topic is what makes you authentic and real, and people connect and engage with real people.

Q I realize that being able to communicate and speak on my feet are very important skills. When it comes to corporate advancement, how would you rate communications as a skill compared to technical skills in one's area of expertise?

A Being able to communicate clearly and in a concise and meaningful way is something people will notice. I'm sure we have all been in the presence of someone who has something worthy of sharing but simply cannot get the message across because their thoughts are all over the place and they can't win their audience's attention long enough to engage them. The result, after they speak, is silence.

There are five Cs in communication that will help you make a positive impression on anyone:

Clarity: Does your message use simple, easy-to-understand language that is free of jargon and acronyms?

Completeness: When you are stating an opinion or perspective, is it balanced to show both sides of the argument? Are you painting the entire picture, or just the half you want to show?

Conciseness: We have two ears and one mouth, which means we should listen twice as much as we speak. Always a good principle to follow! Say what you have to say, but keep it brief and to the point.

Concreteness: Back up your findings with hard facts. Credibility is built on facts, not opinions.

Correctness: I see this as political and cultural correctness. Keep edgy jokes and gossip to yourself.

Q I get really nervous when I have to present an idea to a room full of people. I know you speak of using that nervous energy to work for you, but how do you get over that initial hump to say the first words?

A First rule: don't try to get rid of your nervousness. It's good energy so please don't wish it away. Here are a few techniques that may help you:

1. Speak to a few people in the room ahead of time about some general things (not your topic of presentation and definitely do not tell them you're nervous!). This will get you connecting at a very normal level with others in the room.

2. When you start speaking, start with items you are comfortable with rather than something that requires a great deal of set up. Try to find an item to kick off the meeting that everyone is familiar with or that can trigger some easy discussion. Remember my five-minute rule: once you get past the first five minutes, things will flow better for you.

3. If you still find yourself tripping and getting into a spiral of nervousness, ask a question to get others talking. This will take the attention off you and will give you a chance to compose yourself and get back on track.

Good luck!

Q I tend to over prepare for my presentations. When I visualize my success and feel confident when I get up there, if I mix up one word or the audience doesn't respond the way I visualized, I freeze up and the rest of the presentation is strained and full of nerves. Any advice how to push through if there's a bump at the start?

A I want you to think of presentations as waves in the ocean. They're fluid and can change direction due to the course of the wind. Your presentation too should be fluid. What I suspect is happening is that you are planning precisely every detail down to the punch line. I would recommend you focus your preparation on key areas rather than key words. I would also suspect you are trying to memorize your words, which can be risky since a loss of a word or two can send you into a spiral, racing for these lost words that you've used to connect to other words. I recommend you prepare your presentation by sections:

1. What is your opening about?

2. What is your transition to your first key topic?

3. What do you wish to end your first topic with?

4. What is your transition to your second topic, etc.?

A final word on visualization: what you are visualizing is not your exact words and moves. Instead, you are visualizing a feeling you get when you see yourself delivering with ease. It's that wonderful feeling you get when you know things are going well and people are connecting with you. Feel that as you visualize and imagine that same feeling when you are on stage. May all your bumbling be banished!

Q I'm one of those people who loves presenting! I get a high when I go on stage and get to talk to people. I thought your ideas about presentation preparation were great. Even though I enjoy presenting, I continually want to do better. What's your advice for people wanting to step up their A game?

A It's great to hear you love presenting and you want to get even better. Presentations are one area where you can truly never stop learning. What I would suggest is to watch others present.

There is so much to learn from others. I may watch a program on TV and see someone speak on a topic I have absolutely no interest in but I watch for other things – how they use their hands, how they move on stage, where they look when they speak. Great presenters are all around you – listen and learn.

My Action Steps to Brighter Presentations

The next time I present:

I will "let go" of this type of fear:

_____ (Page 69)

I will be sure to do this in the first five minutes of my presentation:

_____ (Page 72)

I will increase my energy during my delivery by:

_____ (Page 77)

I will make an extra effort to make my content relevant to my audience by:

_____ (Page 80)

My Notes:

Did you know?

Sources:

www.slideshare.net/businessandthegeek/human-resources-employee-engagement-statistics

www.thesocialworkplace.com/2011/08/social-knows-employee-engagement-statistics-august-2011-edition/

Brighter Tomorrows

"If you don't give people information, they'll make up something to fill the void."

— Carla O'Dell, American author and knowledge management expert

Brighter Tomorrows:
Shine in the Face of Change

Why is change such a challenge for people? Have you ever tried to recall all the changes you have gone through in your life? In the last year? How about the last month? It's a pretty daunting task, isn't it? Not only because there are so many changes, but also because it's difficult to determine what in fact constitutes a "change." Does changing your route to work count? How about your gym routine? Your hairstyle? I know it can get pretty ridiculous to think about small and insignificant things as changes. But what may seem small and insignificant to you may be quite different for someone else.

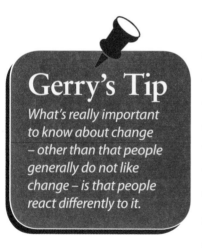

Gerry's Tip

What's really important to know about change – other than that people generally do not like change – is that people react differently to it.

Let me give you an example. I have friends who are notorious for changing plans at the last minute. They will make plans for dinner next Friday night at one of my favourite restaurants, and the Thursday before the dinner, they will call to say someone doesn't like that restaurant or they were just there not too long ago, so they have chosen another location. No big change, right?

Well, yes and no. For my part I *love* the restaurant that was in the original plan and for the entire week I had been thinking about their menu and what I would like to order, given I know it quite well. This change, quite minor and insignificant to them, was not so insignificant to me.

Another example may be something you have experienced yourself. Have you ever shared news of a change with someone, which you considered not a big deal, but discovered that their reaction and what occurred afterwards proved otherwise?

What's really important to know about change – other than that people generally do not like change – is that people react differently to it. And herein lies one of the fundamentals of how we help people through the face of change. Knowing how others perceive change will help you to think and plan your communication beyond your own understanding of that change. We have always been taught to learn to step into or walk a mile in someone else's shoes. Your ability to do this when it comes to change will become invaluable as you work with others in your career.

How do you know how someone is feeling towards change? Ask. The only way to find out is to ask, seek and discover.

Welcome to Grade 4

It's amazing how many misunderstandings could be avoided if only we asked for meaning or clarification. I am often baffled in meetings when an obvious question is just waiting to be asked, but isn't. I don't know when we lose the ability to ask questions, but for me it was somewhere between Grade 4 and 6, when it seemed to become uncool to ask a lot of questions. I still remember the looks I would get from the other kids for asking what

I believed were good questions. Their eyes would roll, secret smirks would be exchanged and at times I even heard a sigh, which I interpreted as: "That is the stupidest question ever, Lewis!" Even when I think about it now, I am transported back in time and can still feel the embarrassment I experienced then. It's a good thing for me that I didn't stop asking questions.

One Statistic I Will Always Remember

 One thing that really helped me was a statistic someone shared with me a long time ago. I'm pretty sure it was a university professor in one of his first classes of the term. He said: "If you have a question, there is a high likelihood that five other people have the exact same question, but are afraid to ask. So do them a favour and ask it first." From that point on, I was never hesitant to ask again.

When it comes to finding out what and how others are feeling about a change so you can help them through it, this principle still applies. If you don't ask, you will never really know what is happening inside their heads. And while they may be nodding in understanding or acceptance, what's going on inside their heads can be quite different. Remember, we are all great actors of "agreement" because we are taught from a very early age to be agreeable.

"Does Anyone Have Any Questions?"

 So how do you ask if no one is willing to share his or her feelings about the change you have introduced? Often supervisors and managers will have a meeting to share information on the change and ends it with a question: "Does anyone have any questions?" I don't know about everyone else, but that always brings me back to Grade 4 and the looks, smirks and sighs. And usually there are no questions, but if someone does ask a question, it is usually about something technical about the change – the date when it starts, what happens to the old forms or processes. This will not give you any insight into how they feel or what they are thinking about this change. Yet, knowing how they feel and think about this change is important. *It gives you insight and perspective other than your own.*

Insight and Perspective

Insight and perspective are the two most powerful tools any leader, manager or supervisor can possess. It's that "aha moment" insight into someone's thinking, and once you can get it, respect it and communicate through it, you will be seen as someone who is empathetic, caring, respectful and respected. These are prerequisites of becoming a good change leader.

What Questions Work Best to Provide Insight and Perspective?
Well, if "Does anyone have any questions?" is not the best way, what is? I often use the "Think, Feel, Do" method to get to understand people. After you introduce the change, here are some questions you can ask:

- What thoughts were going through your head as I was sharing this information with you?

- What are your thoughts now, having heard this?

- How does this make you feel?

- How do you think others will feel about this?

- How will this change what you will be doing?

- How does that make you feel?

- Can you tell me why?

These questions are not meant to be interview-style but rather more conversational and fluid. I use them to start drawing out what people are thinking and feeling. I have always believed that no matter what, people will always know how they feel about something, and how someone feels is worth asking, seeking and discovering. Once you ask these questions, however, you have to *listen*. **And listen without judgment.**

One of the toughest skills is to listen without judging. We've all been there before, when someone is saying something and before they have even finished what they had to say, we already have an opinion of what they just said as well as how we plan to correct or counter it. When we judge, we run the risk of dismissing what we've heard as inaccurate, incorrect or misunderstood by the individual. Our next course of action (before we even finish listening to them) is to prepare our rebuttal.

Listening without judgment means you need to hear the individual's full thought. Even if there are inaccuracies or errors, the intent is not to *correct* but to *connect* with where their perspective comes from.

Listen to learn where they may have come up with this point of view or perspective. You will achieve much greater success at taking someone through change when you approach it from this perspective, rather than defending, arguing or insisting on the change.

How to Get Better at Listening Without Judging During Change

Try Counting to 10

You've probably heard of the "count to 10" rule for not reacting to a contentious statement or challenge. Counting to 10 helps us not to judge as well. By taking the time to count to 10, we are in fact preventing ourselves from *reacting* to the statement or challenge, and allowing ourselves to be in a better position to *respond* to it. When we react, it is usually emotionally driven and more often than not, it's heated, defensive and can at times create what I refer to as a "shutdown" of the individual. In dealing with people and change, shutting down is the last thing you want them to do. You need to hear from them, and often.

Counting to 10 gives you the time to consider *how best to respond.* You need to commit to not reacting, but instead responding to others. This is a great way to listen without judging.

Canvassing Others

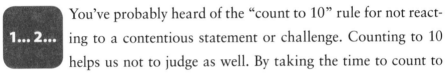

Another way I work at listening without judging is to seek how others are also feeling. My father had a saying he would repeat often: If one person comes up to you to tell you it's a duck, they could be wrong. If another person comes up to you and tells you it's a duck, there may be a chance it is a duck. However, if the third and fourth persons come up and say you have a duck, well then, it is quite likely a duck.

Seeking out other people's perspectives of what you've been told may tell you a great deal about what is happening in their world that you may not be seeing. Recall what I said at the start of this chapter that change affects people differently. When you hear something that strikes you as inconsistent with what you believe or comes across as a negative or even contentious, take the time to explore where this is coming from. What you may be experiencing is resistance to change.

Here are three universal truths when it comes to leading change:

- You can never over-communicate during a time of change

- It is amazing how people can interpret one message in many ways

- Resistance to change will occur

Exploring resistance to change is another great way to gain insight and perspective as a leader. Do not try to avoid or muffle resistance. Doing so will only create an undercurrent of negativity that could swell over time. Resistance should be welcomed, and by this I mean shared in an open, constructive and mutually respective way. People resist change for a number of reasons, but primarily they fall into three categories:

1. They don't know enough about the change

2. They don't have the skills to take them through the change

3. They are not willing to go with the change

The first two categories can be handled with information, training and ongoing communication. The final category is the more challenging one, but not insurmountable. Learning why individuals are not willing or motivated to go with the change will be your key to taking them there. And the best way to learn is by asking questions and listening without judgment.

Counting to 10, canvassing others and getting to the heart of resistance will get you far more insight and perspective than correcting, countering or trying to convince them at this point. Put yourself into the position of: *"I am here to learn, not to judge."* This will put you into the right frame of mind so you are fully prepared to truly listen, and not just hear the words.

Moving from Learning to Leading Change

Congratulate yourself! If you have been able to learn new insights and perspectives from conversations and meetings, you have achieved more than most people who have tried to lead change. Next, what you *do* with these insights and perspectives is even more important. Going from learning to leading is what will help you shine and make people take notice, and earn you respect as a leader.

Think, Feel and Do

 Now that you know what your team members Think, Feel and Do, your next step is to ask yourself: "What would I like them to Think, Feel and Do *after* we go through this change? How would I like them to think about this change taking place? How would I like them to feel? And what do I want them to do differently as a result of this change? Having these clear in your mind is what I call our **Desired State Outcomes for Change**. Having a desired outcome for change lets you know the following:

- How long is the journey from what the team members currently "Think, Feel and Do" to where you would like them to "Think, Feel and Do"?

- Who are the early adopters to change whom you can turn into advocates of change?

- Who are your resistors in the organization and with whom you will need to work?

- Who is sitting on the fence of change? Could they, with some guidance, be turned into advocates who can help move some of the resistors?

Game Plan – From Current State to Desired State Outcomes

How do we go from here to there? Don't let it overwhelm you or stress you out. Think of it like planning a party. You know what you need, but if you think about everything at once, it's like you're planning the Oscars. Like all things in life, it's much easier if you break it down into smaller, more manageable parts. So to get people from here to there, there are six important steps to take them through:

Six Important Steps to Dealing with Change

1. **They need to KNOW what is changing.**

2. **They need to SEE themselves in this change.**

3. **They need to LEARN new skills.**

4. **They need to USE them.**

5. **They need to OWN it.**

6. **They need to FEEL successful.**

1. They Need to KNOW What is Changing

Just because they've heard something once or twice and saw a memo posted online or in the lunchroom, doesn't mean your team necessarily knows what's changing. Think of your communication as a new television show. New programming cannot rely solely on the TV listings. In fact, this is a sure way for it not to be seen. Recall all the ads you see promoting a new program, showing the highlights and reminding you of the day, time and channel. These teasers make you aware and perhaps pique your interest. Think of your change communication in the same way. What can you do to raise everyone's awareness of the change and pique their interest? It may not be nearly as interesting as the TV show but it doesn't need to be. It's all about getting their attention long enough for them to know the change is coming.

"How the 'Rest' was Won": A Case Study About Communicating to Mobilize and Engage People

Sarah and John sat together after their team meeting to strategize about how they could "make it happen." They were facing a challenge because their department was about to join with nine other departments for an all-employee recognition event. In the past, each department held its own event. For the most part, the events were considered successful, with about 50% of employees attending. Now, with 10 departments being brought together for the first time with few people knowing each other, Sarah and John were concerned about a low turnout.

Steve, Sarah and John's boss, was leading this event. He asked them to do whatever they could to ensure they hit at least a 70% registration rate for this event. Without 70% registration, it would be seen as a failure and a waste of money.

Sarah made sure the "Save the Date" communication went out along with the theme of the recognition event: *How the West was Won!*

The event was in eight weeks and online registration was due to open in three weeks. It was already the beginning of July. With vacations at their peak, Sarah thought they should wait until registration opened to see if further promotion was needed.

John thought waiting for three weeks was not a good idea. "We need to get the word out more often and get people wanting to register the day it opens up," he said. He had a plan and convinced Sarah and Steve that it was worth doing.

Over the course of the next three weeks, John and Sarah had one objective: Raise awareness and desire for all 350 employees across 10 departments. Their plan is shown below:

Week	Activities/Communication	Know and See the Change
Week One	Save the date email	Know
Week One	Small poster in the lunchrooms and next to department printers/photocopiers	Know
Weeks One, Two and Three	Reminders of event during Friday staff meetings	Know
Weeks One, Two and Three	Weekly Monday email trivia: Western movies, Western country hits and Western villains and heroes	See
Weeks One, Two and Three	Dress like a cowboy/cowgirl to work on Fridays	See
Weeks One, Two and Three	Western-themed baked goodies	See
Week Three (Friday before the registration opened on Monday)	Walk around and talk up "Don't forget to register"	Know

On Wednesday afternoon, three days into the registration period, Sarah and John were shocked. More than 60% of employees had already registered! By the following week, registration grew to 85%, which exceeded everyone's expectations.

> The event was a complete hit and although it's hard to say for sure which one of the communications teasers worked, the result made all their efforts worthwhile. Needless to say, both Sarah and John were asked to spearhead the next event for all the departments!

Note: Don't underestimate the power of regular communication to get people aware and motivated to take action. From my experience, it's the one thing that demonstrates how important something is. After all, if you don't communicate it, it must not be that important. Perception is reality.

How to Check They KNOW What is Changing

- Periodically, ask different individuals or groups to describe the change that is happening and why it's happening.

- During general meetings or team gatherings, ask supervisors what they are hearing people say about the change that is happening. Welcome resistance and seek ways to understand which of the three categories they are (Don't Know, Lack of Skill or Lack of Will).

---

2. They Need to SEE Themselves in this Change

People are essentially motivated by one of two things in life: To avoid pain or to make a gain. The pain and gain theory has long been known, but it's often overlooked for mobilizing people and teams. Beyond grabbing their attention and interest, how will this change affect them? What's the gain for them? What pain can they avoid? Identifying the pains and gains will help you make it relevant to them and bring them into the change. Otherwise it's merely a change happening "out there" in someone else's backyard. Linking it to *their* gain and *their* pain brings it home to them. Think about pain and gain like this:

- What pain can this change remove for them?

- What pain could result if they do not change?

- What gain do they value?

- What gain will they experience?

How to Check They SEE Themselves in the Change

- Periodically, ask different individuals or groups to hear from them what they are looking forward to with this change. What benefits do they personally see?

- During general meetings or team gatherings, ask supervisors how individuals are responding to the news of change and if they have begun changing their way of working to facilitate this change. Look for patterns and behaviours, as well as attitudes.

---

3. They Need to LEARN New Skills

 Now that the change is known and on people's radar, it's time to begin building the path to success. *They will need to know what to do with the change.* New or upgraded skills will likely be needed. New skills can be tricky for some, and it is at this point in your game plan that you need refer to my "Think, Feel, Do" approach. What are they *thinking* about this change and its impact on them, and how do they *feel* about this? What have they been *doing* up until now and what are you asking them to do differently after the change? Expecting new skills without understanding how people Think, Feel and Do puts your training efforts and dollars to waste. Gaining this understanding will help you link the skills needed and the learning approach required while you create a positive environment to learn, rather than one completed under resentment.

How to Check They Will LEARN Skills for Changing

- If there is training offered, look to see the registration rate and attendance.

- Conduct a post-training survey of individuals to see if they feel the training or skills learned will help them with this change. Do they need more training and if so, what training would be beneficial? Engaging them in new skills acquisition at this stage will help motivate them to take ownership of this change. Encourage learning at all times.

---

4. They Need to USE these Skills

Learning something new and using it regularly is key to successful change. It's like me trying to learn Mandarin. Once the class was over, I stopped using the language and waited until the next class to practise again. This is not a good way to learn! To this day, I can say only one line in Mandarin. That line? "I do not speak well in Mandarin!"

In Malcolm Gladwell's book *The Outliers*, he says: "Researchers have settled on what they believe is the magic number for true expertise: 10,000 hours." I'm not sure we need to spend 10,000 hours, but for something to become a habit, 21 times seems to be the magic number for me. Try doing something 21 times and see if it becomes natural for you to do it.

How to Check They are USING What They Learned

- Periodically, ask different individuals or groups to talk about how their new skills or training has helped them with the change: listen to what is being said as well as what is not.

- During general meetings or team gatherings, ask supervisors what they are observing in terms of skills application. Do they see changes in work patterns, or are old habits and practices surfacing? Application of learning is critical to change success.

---

5. They Need to OWN it

Owning it means they are clear about the change and its impact on them, they are confident they can do it, and they feel competent enough at it to become teachers. This is the stage where you know your efforts have paid off, the change you have been implementing is taking shape, and people and teams are building momentum. This is great news and something you should be very happy about. It's not easy to come this far, but the results will reveal themselves and right about now, people are noticing your ability to lead and effect change. Let's go to the final step: Helping them feel successful.

6. They Need to FEEL Successful

 Tell them about their successes. Show them what gains have been made as a result of their efforts. Recognize them for the steps they have taken. Thank them often. There is nothing more invigorating than knowing you have put in a good day's work. It doesn't matter if it was a long day, week or month, but to see the results and to be recognized and thanked for your efforts – nothing builds momentum more than that!

Game changer: a case study on desired state outcomes

Not too long ago, I was asked to help facilitate a conference about a major change within an organization. This change had already been implemented, but because of the size of the change and the fact that more changes were to come, the organizers saw the need to bring everyone together to discuss the changes and update and motivate everyone for the next round.

At many conferences, the agenda often comes from the key messages and priorities organizers feel are important to deliver. This is a common approach and one still in practice. The challenge I find when you do this is: How do you know that your key messages will be heard? Sure, you can repeat them at the beginning, during and end of the conference, reminding people how important they are to them (and you), but until you have addressed the inner thoughts and concerns people come to the conference with, you have only half their ear.

For this particular conference, the agenda outlined in advance contained some of the new enhancements and benefits that would occur after the change was complete. The agenda was designed to show people all the things that would be "better and improved." After all, who doesn't like "better and improved"?

The organizers knew me well and agreed I would do a small informal focus group – one-on-one interviews with representatives from across the country.

My objective: To get a pulse on what they were Thinking, Feeling and Doing about the changes that had taken place and the changes to come.

After my interviews, I discovered something quite remarkable. I expected resistance to the changes and the inability to see the immediate value of these changes. But I was wrong. What I discovered was they *did* see why these changes needed to occur, and many said, "It was long overdue." They saw the benefits of going in this direction and realized it would take time to adapt to these changes.

I also discovered in my interviews something else: When they understood the need and benefit of these changes, they felt overwhelmed by them. Worse, they did not have any idea of what was coming next. They felt reactive to these changes and in being reactive, they could not manage their teams' concerns and issues with confidence. And in the absence of knowledge about when more changes were coming, and feeling overwhelmed about being able to address concerns from their team members, they felt a rising sense of frustration and helplessness right across the country.

Had we left the original agenda as is, speaking of the great things that were going to happen and the "better and improved" world in the future, we would have completely missed the angst and frustration people brought into the conference. Worse than that, the organizers would have been blindsided had this frustration surfaced during the conference. None of the great things coming would have been heard or seen as "great" given the audience's current state of "Think, Feel and Do."

With a minor rework and repositioning of the agenda, the organizers placed upfront at the start of the conference a heartfelt appreciation of what the audience had experienced in the past year. The organizers shared that they understood how employees felt during this period and knew what their concerns were. When their concerns were listed and addressed in the first 30 minutes of the opening, and they heard a promise that the rest of the conference would focus on dealing with these concerns, we heard a collective sigh, followed by mass applause.

By truly taking the time to understand the audience's *current state of how they* "Think, Feel and Do," we were able to map our way to our **Desired State Outcome** for change in a well-planned, properly executed way – one that addressed their concerns, empowered them to resolve their issues and get them inspired about the future, and one that allowed them to see for themselves a "better and improved future."

After the conference, the first two steps of the Change Game Plan were completed and individuals were ready to learn, apply, own and succeed! This state of readiness is what will fuel us to the **Desired State of Outcomes.**

Recap

Checklist for change: Questions to ask after you Introduce change

☐ What thoughts went through your head as I was sharing this information with you?

☐ What are your thoughts now, having heard this?

☐ How does this make you feel?

☐ How do you think others will feel about this?

☐ How will this change what you will be doing?

☐ How does that make you feel?

☐ Can you tell me why?

Six important steps to dealing with change

1. They need to KNOW what is changing.

2. They need to SEE themselves in this change.

3. They need to LEARN new skills.

4. They need to USE them.

5. They need to OWN it.

6. They need to FEEL successful.

Ask Gerry

Q What's the most important lesson you've learned about communicating change?

A I have always lived by this important lesson: We need to first understand before we can be understood. Taking the time to understand at first seems like a lot of work, and perhaps redundant. After all, you may feel you already "understand." If you always take the position that you are there to learn and not to judge, you will always learn something – always.

When I was 27 years old, I felt I knew all I needed to know about people, life, love and career. When I was 37, I realized I knew much more then than I did at 27. When I turned 47, it dawned on me I knew only a fraction of what I did when I was 27 and my assumptions then … well, were mostly wrong. My learning at 50 is that I am always going to be learning and that what I hold to be unchangeable truths of the universe can and will be changed.

Q How do you help people own change?

A People change at their own pace and what feels right to them, but there is nothing more motivating than results. When people see they have achieved small successes, they will drive themselves toward bigger successes. We're programmed this way but all too often, we minimize our own successes (and those of others) and seek to point out only how much farther we need to go. Take stock, look back and see how far you've come. As a leader, you want to help someone build a momentum that can't be stopped. Keep moving forward.

Q How do you make change "stick"?

A Be the change. And not just drive the change. Your actions, re-actions and non-verbal gestures are what people will read and hear much louder than what you say. It begins with you and how much you believe the change is important, necessary and positive. Once you have set your own course for change, find others who can help you champion it. These are the change champions who will make it a point to find the positives, solve the negatives, unblock the barriers and truly live the quote "where there is a will, there is a way."

Q What should I communicate?

A Change champions need to communicate regularly to every-one and not just those who are for the change. They need to illustrate the four key areas that are important to keep everyone on board through the change:

1. Where are we with the change?

2. What issues have been raised? Have we solved them?

3. What have we achieved?

4. What's next?

Keeping everyone updated on these four key areas will create the mass momentum you'll need for successful and lasting change.

Q I recognize that it is important to adapt to change within a company, but my firm seems to be changing key systems every year. Why should I believe this time is any more permanent? How do I get decision-makers to understand that if they listened to us in the first place, we wouldn't need to be asked for change yet again?

A While I cannot speak for your company, I can speak about change. The sooner you get comfortable with change, the more comfortable you will be and quite honestly, the better you will be seen as a change agent and not as a change barrier. I empathize with you that change often leads to more work and having to re-learn things. I am a proponent of learning new things so perhaps if we can shift our attitudes to lead the change vs. be led by change, we might be able to manage transitions more quickly and easily.

✓ My Action Steps to Brighter Tomorrows

The next time I lead people through change:

I will use this question to gain better insight and perspective on the change that is happening:

_____ (Page 117)

I will get more people to buy into change by remembering this step in my change game plan:

_____ (Page 122)

My Notes:

Brighter Connections and Relationships

"*People will forget what you said. People will forget what you did. But people will never forget how you made them feel.*"

— Maya Angelou, American poet, actor and civil rights activist

Brighter Connections and Relationships:
Be the Bright Light Others Seek Out

"If you want to go somewhere, it is best to find someone who has already been there."

— Robert Kiyosaki, American investor, businessman and self-help author

Why connect? Life is about relationships. It's as simple as that. Very little, if at all, happens in a vacuum and without some type of interaction. Life, business and love are all about building strong relationships that help you grow, find your path, get back on track if necessary, and discover who you are. Relationships are the mirrors to who we are and who we can become. We learn from good ones and bad ones. The key is *to learn from them*. Seek out relationships, respect them and nurture them. They will become your most valuable tool in creating a shining career.

People often ask me, "How do you network?" When I say I don't network, they always give me a very shocked look. Let me explain. The term "networking" has come to mean gathering the names and contact details of people with whom we want to maintain some connection for mutual business benefit. Nothing is wrong with that. Nothing at all. But for me, it's not about "mutual business benefit." The term "networking" has the word "work" in it. I don't like to work at getting to know people. I would rather enjoy the process and just get to know interesting people –

what's interesting about them, and what's happening in their lives and in their work. When I get to know people with that in mind, it's enjoyable and interesting. Something or nothing may come of it, but that was never the point.

So let me share a term I prefer: *connecting.* I love connecting with people. The whole idea of connecting means you are focused on that individual – not like at a cocktail party when someone is talking to you, but you can tell they're scouring the room to see who they want to move to next. Connecting means you are focused, attentive and interested. No one will be interested in getting to know you if you're not interested in them.

I have been very fortunate to be able to connect with people not only in North America but also in more than 40 countries around the world. I'll share with you how I connect with people and have learned many important lessons in doing so, mostly from them teaching me some wonderful lessons about relationships.

Gerry's Tip

Stop networking and start connecting. Connecting means you are focused, attentive and interested in the other person.

How Do I Start Connecting?

Smile. It doesn't matter what language you speak or what culture you are from. A smile is universal, yet we don't do it enough. Why don't we smile? As I've traveled around the world, I've noticed smiling is easier for some people than for others. In my experience, the world is made up of three kinds of faces. One-third of people have a face that almost always seems to look cheerful. These are the lucky ones because they are the easiest to start a smile. You probably know people who naturally appear happy, pleasant and even have "smiling eyes." They are the ones who have this type of face – happy faces.

The next third are the neutral faces. Their lip line is relatively straight and in some ways they are expressionless until triggered by something internal or external. They can definitely smile, but it takes more work and more of a conscious effort. If you have one of these faces, know that you have to think happy thoughts to create a smile. If you don't consciously make this happen, the look you have is one of neutrality and quite possibly disinterest.

The final third are the serious faces. You know who they are. These types often have a hard time smiling for the camera. You tell them to smile and they say, "but I *am* smiling!" Serious faces need serious practice to smile.

All three faces are capable of smiling, but two of the three just need more of a conscious effort.

This takes practice. Don't think just because you think you are smiling, that in fact you are. Take a look in the mirror when you have a chance or ask a friend. If you're in doubt about your smile, think of something that makes you really happy and feel, not just see, if the expression on your face has changed. Now *that's* the smile that people will warm up to.

Smiling will definitely make you more approachable and friendlier, and someone people are more willing to meet.

Now that you have the smile down, what's next?

You Had Me at "Hello"

 A client of mine used to say this to me and it always made me smile. "Hello" is the next thing we need to convey a connection. Not "Hi, my name is Gerry, I'm in communications." This comes later – much later. Connecting requires taking the first step and "Hello" is the best place to start.

The combination of a smile, good eye contact and a genuine "hello" lays the foundation to connect. At many events, I notice people standing to the sides looking to see if anyone comes up to them. Or if they walk around, they do so with their eyes searching the room as if they are looking for someone.

When you're at an event, try simply walking around, enjoying the scenery of people in front of you. Take your time, listen to what's happening and just appreciate the stroll. Eventually you'll make eye contact with someone. Smile. Say hello. See what happens. Rushing this process or trying too hard is where most people fail. It's not a game of "tag, you're it." Think of it as "Let me count how many people are here." (But don't count out loud or even silently; it's just a way to slow your eyes down and gives you something to do.)

> **Gerry's Tip**
>
> The combination of a smile, good eye contact and a genuine 'hello' lays the foundation to connect.

When you do make eye contact, smile and say hello. This is the time to see if you are able to connect into a conversation. It may not happen but what you do next will determine that.

Gerry's Tip

Being interested is one of the best ways to begin a conversation as well as to connect with people.

Conversation Starters

This topic reminds me of the old days of dating when I first started going to bars and clubs to meet people, and the struggles I had to start a conversation. I say the old days because today, this whole process now begins with an emoticon – or worse, with a "hey" in the chat box.

We're talking about connecting here, and conversations still happen and *need to happen*.

There are no great one-liners to start a conversation and the more you try to think of one, the worse it will be for you. How to approach starting a conversation is to think why you and the individual are here to begin with. Is it a conference, a business meeting, a social event or just sheer coincidence? Start with why you are there in the same place and ask them about the event.

Here are some examples:

- How do you like (the event) so far?

- What do you think about (describe something that happened at the event)?

- How did you feel about (describe something that happened at the event)?

Do you see how I've incorporated the *Think, Feel, Do* approach here to start the conversation?

These questions are merely suggestions, but there is a purpose behind them; that is, you should be interested in what the other person has to say. Being interested is one of the best ways to begin a conversation as well as to connect with people. One of the very first things I learned about building relationships is that it is far more important to be interested than to be interesting. We are all very good at talking about us; I even catch myself doing this sometimes. It's definitely easier to talk about ourselves than to get other people to talk about themselves, but the effort is well worth it. You learn more, connect better and leave a much stronger and more lasting impression.

Building relationships starts with connecting – meeting lots of people and getting to know them, and them getting to know you and remember you. Recall what I said about relationships at the top of this chapter: relationships help you grow, find your path, get you back on track and help you discover who you are.

Let's build from our foundation now and make the assumption you have started a nice conversation and are enjoying exchanging meaningful dialogue. That's great work! You're connecting with people and are already shining brighter.

Eight Lessons for Successful Connections

I've been connecting with people and building relationships for as long as I can remember. Having traveled extensively for work, I had the great opportunity to learn about building relationships across borders, in different languages and diverse cultures. What have I learned? That the fundamentals of building great connections that lead to relationships are universal. And that people are people despite where they are from and their language of preference. We are all human and as humans, we appreciate and value many similar things in who we connect with. What follows next are my eight universal lessons for building strong connected relationships.

1. Smile

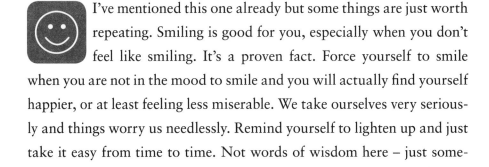

I've mentioned this one already but some things are just worth repeating. Smiling is good for you, especially when you don't feel like smiling. It's a proven fact. Force yourself to smile when you are not in the mood to smile and you will actually find yourself happier, or at least feeling less miserable. We take ourselves very seriously and things worry us needlessly. Remind yourself to lighten up and just take it easy from time to time. Not words of wisdom here – just something I practise and hope to pass along. Be happy. Smile more. And here's my favourite: Smile at someone you don't know today – make their day!

2. Be Interested

I saw this for the very first time in Dale Carnegie's book *How to Win Friends and Influence People*. As a kid, I hung around bookstores all the time, in the days before Chapters or Indigo existed, welcoming us to plop down in a comfy chair. I would sit in the aisle of the Coles bookstore reading books on end and being fascinated by what books could teach me.

One of the most influential books for me was Dale Carnegie's, even though I didn't truly understand that lesson until much later in life. His lesson — that it is more important to "be interested than to be interesting" — is one of my core beliefs when it comes to building relationships.

Connections and relationships are very much about being remembered. You want to be in someone's mental database so when they need something, they connect with you as someone who can help them.

Being genuinely interested means asking without being intrusive. How do you tell the difference? Ask yourself why you want to know. If it's because you do care and want to help, you're likely to be interested. If you answer, "Because I'm curious," you may be intrusive. And if ever in doubt, ask them: "Am I being intrusive?"

Gerry's Tip

Connections and relationships are very much about being remembered.

Allowing others to speak and share with you is the greatest form of flattery and should always be respected. I've learned to never share information I've been asked not to share. "Just between you and me" means "just between you and me." Being known as someone who can be responsible with information is valuable and builds incredible trust. I don't need to tell you what happens when the opposite happens, other than to say it's not a good thing.

Here's one final thought on being interested: Learn from what they tell you. Remember things that are important to others. It may not seem important to you at the time, but it's always amazing to me when people remember the little things. It personalizes connections and creates memorable relationships. You will be remembered.

3. Say My Name

 Beyoncé's hit song said it all. People love their names being said and the fact you can remember their name is *priceless.* Saying someone's name is the sweetest sound – in any language.

"But I am terrible at remembering names!" This is the most common remark I hear from people. Yes, it is difficult but there are ways to become better at this. I use the following techniques and for the most part, I have gotten better at this over the years.

Remembering someone's name at an event is different from recalling a name the next time you meet them – the latter being more challenging – but they both have the same starting points.

Repeat it: Repetition helps. Repeat their name.

JENNIFER:
Hi, my name is Jennifer.

YOU:
Hello Jennifer, nice to meet you.

Spell it (in your head): When you repeat their name, make a conscious effort to visualize the spelling in your head. See the name on one of those "Hello My Name is" tags. Yes, this works.

Use it: At least three times in the next 90 seconds.

JENNIFER:
Hi, my name is Jennifer.

YOU:
Hello *Jennifer*, nice to meet you.

YOU:
Jennifer, what do you think of the event so far?
OR
YOU:
Jennifer, let me introduce you to my friend Alice, Alice this is *Jennifer*. We just met at the conference today.

Link it: Think of someone you know who has the same name. In your head, this link will help you remember their name more easily.

Sound it: If it's a name that is difficult to remember or say, people will not mind you working hard to pronounce their name. In fact, they will appreciate you are trying to get it right rather than gloss over it or butcher it like many do. Ask them, "Help me pronounce your name." They will most likely phoneticize their name and break it into parts for you. This will help you. Just remember to use it often in the next 90 seconds to anchor that sound in your head.

Don't do this! Once, a long time ago, I tried to cheat the situation and said to someone: "Sorry, I don't remember your name. I remember it had an unusual spelling." He said: "My name is John. J – O –H – N." I can laugh about it now!

Rhyme it: It may also help to rhyme their name with another word. I once met someone named Juiling (Jiow-ling) and it was next to impossible to pronounce it until he said "My name sounds like 'bowling'" and I have never forgotten it since!

Remembering someone's name the next time you see them is more challenging. However, if you have made a connection and kept in touch, this will not be an issue. If it is someone you have not kept in touch with, try this method:

Recall it: Think of where you met them. Usually the location will trigger the conversation. Recall what you may have spoken about and the name should pop up. Don't force it; just recall the pleasant conversation you had.

If that does not work, try a very simple statement like: "Hi, it's great to see you again. I'm sorry, I cannot seem to recall your name just now." I like saying "I can't seem to recall your name" because it sounds much better than "Sorry, I cannot remember your name." Also, saying you cannot "recall" means you have made the effort to do so; this alone is impressive.

4. Listen, Really Listen

 Multi-tasking has been revered as a great trait and admired as a key competency in most, if not all, organizations. However, multi-listening, that is, listening to the individual speaking as well as your own inner thoughts, is neither admirable nor productive. It's not entirely your fault, though. We have a lot going on every day and with the onslaught of mobile devices and instant access, keeping your thoughts focused is nearly impossible. However, not paying attention to your connections is costly. Let me be perfectly clear: people know when you are not paying attention to what they are saying. I have seen more off-somewhere-else looks than I care to count. Then there is the fact that we have never truly been taught to listen. We've been told to pay attention as kids, but no one teaches you to be a good listener.

I don't profess to be a "listening coach" but I do have three self-imposed rules to help me stay focused on one person and the conversation I am having with them.

- *Don't interrupt or cut them off* (easier said than done). By not jumping in, you are letting their entire message come out. You can nod, smile, even laugh to show agreement or great enjoyment. But try not to add to the conversation at the cost of theirs. The next time you find yourself cutting someone off, stop yourself. It's a good practice and will be appreciated.

- *Look at them.* Seems obvious, doesn't it? You'd be surprised how many conversations I have had where people are not looking at me. Instead they look over my shoulders (as if they see someone else), they look at their mobile device (with the occasional grunt of acknowledgement – thanks!), or they look in my general direction but their eyes tell me they are thinking about something completely different. I call this the vacant look or distracted look. Eye contact with frequent acknowledgement tells me you are listening and engaged.

- *Listen for key words.* As someone is speaking, listen for words that will help you remember the conversation later, like the headlines of a story. This is not selective listening, but rather a way to help you capture the essence of what was said. Think of it as hitting "like"on Facebook each time you hear a key word.

Your ability to listen well will give you two gifts: connectedness and recall. In other words, you will be able to demonstrate you are truly connected and engaged in the conversation. This proves to the person you're talking to that he or she is the *most* important person at that moment.

Being able to recall will also impress others. When you remember things that are important to them, you demonstrate that you value what they shared with you. Who doesn't want to feel valued and paid attention to? Need I say more? Next time you catch yourself breaking my three listening rules, stop yourself and start again. No one will catch on and you can start clean without them even knowing you broke them. Awareness is a very powerful tool.

5. Integrity

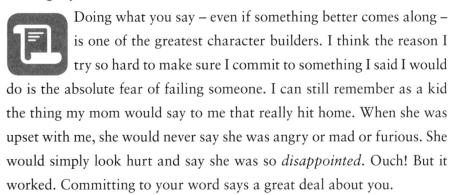

Doing what you say – even if something better comes along – is one of the greatest character builders. I think the reason I try so hard to make sure I commit to something I said I would do is the absolute fear of failing someone. I can still remember as a kid the thing my mom would say to me that really hit home. When she was upset with me, she would never say she was angry or mad or furious. She would simply look hurt and say she was so *disappointed*. Ouch! But it worked. Committing to your word says a great deal about you.

People use the following phrase quite often: "under-promise, but over-deliver." While that, too, is effective, I like to keep it simpler: *If you say something, mean it and do it.* Integrity is invisible but is worth its weight in gold. You may not get immediate feedback on your integrity, but trust me, being known as someone who has integrity and gets things done is what will help you get known and remembered.

6. Remove "I" and Use "We"

There's a great Chinese proverb that states: "If you're a flower, you will have a sweet fragrance." In other words, if you're good, people will know. Excellence travels well, so there's no need to broadcast, promote or beat your chest. Rather, say how you achieved success "as a team." Recognizing others and their contribution doesn't diminish your talents. Quite the contrary, it shows how you can work well in a team environment and perhaps even lead a team to success. My mom used to tell my brother: "Self praise, no raise." Gosh, she is a bright lady!

The next time you catch yourself saying "I," simply substitute it with "we." This is a simple switch but one with many longer-term benefits.

7. Have Conviction in Your Ideas

Nothing in life is 100% precise or guaranteed. That's the beauty of it. When you think you have it down, life changes and we need to adjust again. So when you want to share an idea you believe in, but you're not sure if it's absolutely perfect, trust your instincts and be guided by your passion, not your fear. The conviction you have in your own ideas says a lot about you to others. Sure, you can make mistakes – we all do – but I'd rather make a mistake in trying than be too timid to make a move. No one ever won a race by not moving.

In the business of strategy, I find more often than not I am removing fear and instilling confidence in my clients. I believe that if we build things with the right people at the table, with genuine intention to improve, and with respect for the people to whom we deliver, it will always be a good product. Make sure you believe in your ideas and show it in your face, in your body language and in what you say to others.

8. Thank Them

Every time someone sends me a thank you note, it means a lot to me. Taking the time to say thank you is your best way to build connected relationships. On accepting his award for best actor during the Oscars, Matthew McConaughey said: "Gratitude is reciprocal." I could not agree more. Showing gratitude will generate more great things and will keep you humble.

Final Thoughts

 Relationships are essential in life. They help you grow, find your path, get you back on track and also help you discover who you are.

I hope these eight lessons I have learned along the way will help you build strong, lasting and incredibly wonderful relationships in work and in life. Become the bright light that others seek out when they need help. Be true to your connections, respect the relationships you worked so hard to build and you will be valued and remembered. These lessons have helped and continue to help me and I would like to say "Thank you" to all who have taught me along the way.

Recap

Suggested conversation starters

How do you like [the event] so far?

What do you think about [describe something that happened at the event]?

How did you feel about [describe something that happened at the event]?

Eight lessons for successful connections

1. Smile

2. Be interested

3. Say my name

4. Listen, really listen

5. Integrity

6. Remove "I" and use "we"

7. Have conviction in your ideas

8. Thank them

Ask Gerry

Q I really like your idea of connecting with people, instead of just networking with them. In the online world of Facebook and LinkedIn, we are accustomed to thinking the more friends you have, the better. Are there a certain number of connections that you should be striving to achieve? How do you ensure you are making "good" personal connections?

A I believe you should have as many connections as you can invest time in managing. You're absolutely correct: it's not a numbers game and it's not a competition. I know people who are so proud of their many connections, but I know for a fact they have not communicated with them in many years. They are no longer connections, but people you once knew. There is a difference. Connections are people who will make time for you, even if it's just to listen. To have these connections, like any relationship, you have to nurture them and find ways to connect. Let's face it, we all have busy lives and it's not easy to invest time, so choose people for whom you will always want to find time. Those are the ones you should invest your time and energy in.

Q What happens when you run out of things to say? I've had some really awkward quiet moments during a group dinner and the table suddenly went silent.

A Ah, yes – the very long awkward silence. I would first gauge the atmosphere of the table. Sometimes people are enjoying their food and surroundings so much that they are quite happy to have some peaceful eating time. So don't feel you have to start up a conversation every time there is silence. Remember, silence can be golden. If, however, you sense everyone is feeling awkward about the silence they do not know how to break, something I do is to toss a general question. I like general questions because it doesn't put anyone on the spot. I would never say "So, Mary, tell me about that trip you just returned from." Mary may not want to share about her trip and now you've put her on the spot, or worse yet, she gives you a two-word answer. Instead I would ask, "Has anyone gone away recently? I've been trying to come up with a few interesting places to visit next month." Inevitably someone will share places they have visited and enjoyed and it most likely won't even be recently. Generic questions that involve travel, entertainment and food are easy "toss out" questions that can generate some fun conversations around the table.

Q Any tips Dos and Don'ts for business card exchanges?

A First of all, take time to read the card and do not stuff it in your pocket, wallet or purse. Use the time while you're reviewing it to remember the person's name. Find something on the card to start a conversation: job title, location of office, design of card or name of company. Make it a practice every time you look at a card to find something to start a conversation with. Another "Do" would be to mark on the card when you get back as to when you met the person. I keep all my cards even though I transfer them to my contacts. I keep them because every once in a while I will go through my decks of cards (and I have many) but inevitably I find a card that prompts me to reach out. Sometimes nothing comes of it, but I'd say more often than not, an exchange of email usually ensues. When my contacts do respond, I have always found them to be a good investment of my time – not to mention, it's always nice to let people know you remember them. People remember these small surprises and again, you're doing this for no other reason than to keep the connection alive.

✓ My Action Steps to Brighter Connections and Relationships

The next time I'm networking:

My goal will be to:

_____ (Page 141)

One conversation starter that I'll use is:

_____ (Page 144)

When I'm listening to someone I will focus on:

_____ (Page 151)

My Notes:

_____

_____

_____

_____

_____

_____

_____

_____

_____

_____

_____

_____

Brighter Thoughts

"There is little difference in people, but that little difference makes a big difference. The little difference is attitude. The big difference is whether it is positive or negative."

— W. Clement Stone, American businessperson and philanthropist

Brighter Thoughts:
Attitudes Will Determine Your Altitude in Life and in Your Career

"Happiness is an attitude. We either make ourselves miserable, or happy and strong. The amount of work is the same."

— Francesca Reigler, American artist

 Sometimes I think if I had a personal brand, it would be a smiley face. Why? Because when I see one, I can't help but smile inside. It's like when a baby smiles at you – you can't resist smiling back. That's how I have chosen to live. And that's the operative word – chosen. When you think about it, while we would like to control things that happen to us in our lives, it really comes down to one thing that is ultimately within our control: our thoughts.

I've always chosen to look at things with a positive slant – in other words, I see the glass as half full. As cliché as that sounds, I do not like the other choice and so I choose the half-full perspective.

But don't misunderstand this as some Pollyanna approach to the way I see the world. There are plenty of negative things happening in the world, and there always will be. There are plenty of days when my smiley face icon is just a half smile, and yes, on some days, even just a smirk. The most important thing for me is the effort to keep smiling and carrying on with that light just above me – the little "shine" that I keep with me.

People often ask me: "Why are you always so positive, so happy?" I should start by correcting those who think I'm always happy. This is not the case. No one is happy all the time. And I, for one, do have moments and days when I feel like I am in a rut and in a state of overcast. However, the difference with me is that I work towards clearing the clouds and not letting them hang around for long. I acknowledge them and find out why they are there – what I refer to in this book as "deconstructing" – getting to the heart of the cloud and dealing with it. This is all about the strength of mind to take back control of my thoughts and in doing so, my attitude.

When I'm feeling down, I use reinforcement to regain my brighter perspective. A change of scenery helps. As well, simply looking at something can turn my thoughts around. In my office across from my desk are things that make me remember a good place – somewhere, someone, something that made me shine inside and out. I call these my personal touchstones. They bring me back to a state of mind where I am strong or a time when I brightened something, or they touch a personal side of my life I feel blessed to be a part of.

Do not take this lightly or dismiss the importance of reminders. I think we can, if we had to, remember a moment in our childhood that we call our happiest moment or day. I also think we can recall a moment of embarrassment in our lives and if we thought about it this very second, we would feel as though it has just happened. The brain is very powerful and can transport us to moments of sheer happiness and to those we'd rather forget. Touchstones, as I call them, serve the same purpose. They bring me back to a state of centredness – a restart or reboot, if you will. Since life doesn't have an undo button, this is the closest I can get to a restart.

THOUGHT LEADS TO ATTITUDE LEADS TO BEHAVIOUR LEADS TO ACTIONS

Thoughts lead to attitude and attitude leads to behaviour. Behaviours lead to our ultimate action. So it's no surprise that attitude is a key component of success. However, when I look around me, I'm often reminded that many people either don't demonstrate good (let alone great) attitude, and still many more don't make it an everyday practice.

Positive attitude goes far beyond just "good" for us, though. I think it is *the* driving force for success in life and in work. How you look at and interpret what happens around you will determine your next actions. Yes, it is that powerful, and that's why I am convinced attitude is the driving force of our success.

A positive attitude is one of those things we know is good for us – like drinking eight glasses of water a day – but for many reasons, we get side-tracked. We forget just how important it is and we allow life to take us down paths we'd rather not go along, where we see clouds looming ahead.

What I hope to share with you is this:

- You control your own thoughts.

- Your thoughts determine your attitude.

- You can retrain your brain to recognize the attitude, identify the source, deal with the culprit, and move forward.

This is not lying to yourself, but reprogramming your brain. Let's look at a story of "attitude in action."

Janice's Story

Janice manages a team of eight service representatives for a cell phone company. She started this job after her kids reached school age and she had more time to do what she loved: training reps on how to provide excellent customer service. She enjoyed her job and did quite well, with strong performance reviews every year, plus incentive bonuses when her team exceeded the targets set by head office.

In the last year, Janice applied for two positions that are more senior and would involve more people management. In each case, her manager informed her she did not get the position because the successful candidate, while less experienced, had higher qualifications.

Like anyone who was turned down for a position, Janice felt defeated and began listening to an inner voice telling her she should have gone back to school to do her MBA. She spotted another job that interested her, but decided not to apply, fearing the same rejection.

Her job over the next few months began to suffer. She felt bored and unrecognized for what she accomplished. Her team noticed she no longer held her sales rally meetings, which they loved, because Janice always made them fun and competitive.

Because she didn't want to rock the boat, Janice never pursued further why her experience did not stack up against the qualifications the other candidates had on paper. After all, she thought, maybe they were more qualified and smarter than she was. She realized she was thinking about this loss all the time and it was beginning to make her look at her job differently. Maybe it was time for a change, she thought.

The next week, the organization announced they were bringing in a consulting firm to help them enhance the overall customer experience and to seek ways to improve sales and productivity. Janice's manager asked her to help the consultant out by showing him her process as part of their assessment. That night, Janice began thinking this was not good sign.. First, she did not have the right "qualifications," and now she would be under the consultant's microscope. Why would they question how she did things? Did they not think she had a good process in place? Would these "enhancements" mean she would have to change what she did things? Why would she have to change? Janice did not sleep all night.

What Does Janice's Story Tell Us?

The situation Janice experienced and how she felt are not uncommon. There are many unanswered questions for her and for us as to why she didn't get the job, and why the consulting firm is speaking with her. If she were to sit down with her manager and ask some of these important questions, Janice would likely be in a much better place. The essence of this story is not about Janice's not finding out the answers to her questions, but more about how Janice is interpreting what is happening to her and what she is allowing the interpretation to do to her. Her inside view of her world right now is not good and her attitude reflects this, and most likely so will her behaviour and her actions when she goes into work the next day.

We all want to have a good attitude. We don't wake up in the morning convinced that today we're going to have a bad attitude, and dislike what we do and the people with whom we interact. Or that we will be dissatisfied with aspects of our life. We *want* to feel good about all these things. However, as you can see from Janice's story, sometimes we allow our inner voice to control our thoughts and in turn, this affects the way we interpret what is happening to and around us.

The Five Culprits of Negative Attitudes (and How to Conquer Them!)

Let's explore the culprits that lead to poor attitudes. Understanding them is the first step towards identifying why we sometimes feel the way we do and more importantly how we can "snap out of it"! And while this sounds easier said than done, you will be amazed at what you can train your mind to do! Here's what to focus on:

1. **Confidence Crushers**

2. **Concern**

3. **Complacency**

4. Conflict

5. Change

1. Confidence Crushers

A lack of confidence is one of the key reasons people feel bad about themselves, often resulting in a poor attitude. Confidence, however, is something that cannot be taught but only learned through successful experiences. No matter how much you try to tell people to be confident or to believe in themselves more, confidence is one of those things they have to believe in before they can get there. So how do we get there? What do we need to do to build confidence and in turn have a great attitude?

Steve's Story

Steve is a project manager in a large government organization. He excels at what he does. Whenever a department needs to launch a new initiative, they always ask for Steve because his projects are always on time and on budget, and he knows how to lead. He has received so much praise from departments that for their annual conference, the organizers decided to dedicate a workshop to project management excellence. Who better to present than Steve?

When his vice-president approached him, Steve agreed, but he was already feeling sick inside about having to present in front of more than 600 people. He had never spoken in front of so many people before and with every minute, as he prepared for his presentation, he became more and more concerned about his expertise and began questioning himself on whether he was the best person to speak.

How Does Steve Build Confidence?

 As we've mentioned, Malcolm Gladwell says we need 10,000 hours of practice for true expertise. For Steve, and for any of us for that matter, this would be almost impossible. How could he be expected to get 10,000 hours of experience?

After speaking with his vice-president about his concerns, Steve was reassured that he was in fact the best person to speak at the conference. He had led the greatest number of projects for the company and everyone loved his process and the way he communicated to engage all team members. Steve and the vice-president agreed to meet again after Steve prepared his session so his vice-president would give him some feedback.

A week later, Steve returned and after a few rehearsals with his vice-president, believed he had the content under control. He was still extremely nervous presenting. He felt his voice was too high, he spoke way too fast for human comprehension, and he didn't know where to look, so he focused the whole time on his notes even though he knew this material in his sleep.

"How will I get over this?" Steve asked his VP. "I feel like I've never spoken about this topic before! How can I get more comfortable? I know I don't sound confident!"

His VP asked him to use visualization that evening at home, sitting in a quiet place without interruption. In the section of this book on Brighter Presentations, I described how to use creative visualization. To "see" his success, Steve could employ the same technique. Here's a condensed version of the steps involved:

 Visualize yourself at the conference, chatting with your colleagues, feeling great around people you've worked with.

 See yourself sitting at the table as they introduce you. You're smiling as you look around the room and catch the eyes of some of your biggest fans.

 Visualize yourself walking up to the stage, taking a deep breath, smiling, and shaking the hand of the person who introduced you. Sense how your notes feel as you place them on the lectern. See yourself taking a sip of cool water. Feel the slide remote in your hand as you walk to the centre of the stage.

 Visualize the audience as you take five seconds to say "good morning" and then open your talk with an engaging story. Hear the audience responding positively to your story and listening carefully as you continue talking about project planning. Notice the audience writing down your best tips.

Visualize your delivery: see yourself explaining the information clearly, at a slow pace. Notice how your hands gesture naturally and you use your tone and pace to emphasize key points. Visualize someone asking a question and you answering clearly and confidently. Watch the audience nod in agreement.

 Visualize your closing as you share the summary points and your favourite quote on this topic. See yourself thanking the audience and then accepting their thunderous applause.

Visualization is one of the most powerful techniques to reach those "10,000 hours of practice." It can comprise seeing, hearing, feeling and even tasting. Using all your senses as you visualize an experience trains your brain as though you were actually doing it, and doing it extremely well! Practise this technique with anything you want to become better at and see for yourself how powerful it is and why athletes have been doing this for years with incredible success. Seeing something in your mind's eye works.

By the way, Steve rocked it! Not only did his attitude about his ability to present change, but more importantly, he also changed the way he felt about himself as a communicator and boosted his confidence to be in front of one person or 1,000 people.

2. Concern

Over-emphasis on worrying and ongoing fears of "what *could* happen" will affect your attitude negatively as well. Why do we worry? What prevents us from moving on and accomplishing what we need to do? Research tells us that 90% of what we worry about never happens.

Think of the last time you were worried about something. Was it as bad as you imagined it to be? Most likely not. Our ability to stop worrying and get things done is what gives us a sense of accomplishment and achievement. Think about it: there is nothing more empowering than crossing something off your To-Do list.

There are an infinite number of To-Dos in life; if we can just get it done rather than thinking about it — or worse yet, worrying about it — the better we will feel, the stronger we will be and the more positive our attitude.

Alysha's Story

Alysha works as an event co-ordinator for an international organization. Her role involves planning, communicating and executing training programs overseas. Her responsibilities are numerous but she has been doing this for five years and has a good process in place. One of the most challenging parts of Alysha's job is to manage requests and requirements for overseas participants, and much of her work is done through email and conference calls. Because the success of programs requires precise planning and execution, Alysha tends to be extremely stressed and concerned about two months before every program. In fact, she does not sleep for about one week before the program and often gets to the event looking exhausted and agitated, even before the participants have arrived.

She loves what she does but she will be the first to tell you she doesn't know how much longer she can deal with the stress of the job and what goes through her mind with each program.

How Do We Conquer Concern for Alysha?

 Alysha's challenge is that she feels like she is juggling elephants and that if any one of these "elephants" drops – well, you can visualize this, I'm sure.

Alysha needs to learn how to better manage what she can do and let go of what she has no control over.

What Alysha Did

Alysha's director, Donna, sat her down just before the start of the program. Seeing Alysha was looking tired, frustrated and on edge, she knew Alysha needed help. Donna liked Alysha because she was a go-getter and was excellent at solving problems as they happen – the true mark of an events professional.

Donna asked Alysha if she knew the difference between a worrier and a warrior. Alysha looked puzzled but was distracted with yet another concern she had on her mind. Here's what Donna shared with Alysha to help her:

> Our capacity to worry is something unique to being human. While animals have one of two choices in nature – fight or flight – we have the wonderful ability to think. However, with thinking comes the opportunity to worry about the future. Warriors, on the other hand, stand strong on what they can and cannot control. When they cannot control something, they will "let it go." The warrior's attention is focused then on what he or she *can* control, placing attention on getting things done.

Donna asked Alysha to write down a list of all the things she was worried about or that caused her concern. Alysha at first didn't know where to start so Donna asked her, "What keeps you up at night when you think about the programs you are about to run?" This became clearer for Alysha, so she started listing all the things she lay awake thinking about before programs. Here is a list of what she came up with:

1. *Incomplete immigration papers from participants that could turn them back at Customs*

2. *Participants' flight delays and missed connecting flights*

3. *Hotel not attentive to food restrictions and allergies of participants*

4. *Participants' materials lost during transit*

5. *Ground transportation to get all participants to the hotel on time for the start of the program*

6. *Making sure she has the latest version of speakers' presentations*

The list went on, but this was enough for Donna to help Alysha think through the worrier vs. warrior exercise. Donna asked Alysha to look at her list and select those items she has absolutely no control over. Alysha at first thought she had control over every one of them, but Donna insisted she think about this more carefully. Alysha finally conceded that items 2 and 4 were completely out of her hands. Flight delays and lost materials are common and in the event they happened (and they do happen), Alysha had always found a workaround.

The remaining items – particularly 1, 3, 5 and 6 – were about Alysha's ability to communicate well and having a good system to monitor the status of each item. As long as Alysha managed and tracked correspondence and kept an updated file in her computer, she should be confident that all necessary measures have been taken to prevent mistakes.

Donna was able to help Alysha understand and act on the areas within her control and to let go of the areas she cannot control. This takes practice and is often easier said than done. However, the more we focus on being a warrior and the less on worrying, the more likely we are to be in control of any situation and the less likely we are to be depleted.

Gerry's Tip

"Let it go" are three words that should be in everyone's daily mantra to help them secure a positive and productive attitude.

"Let it go" are three words that should be in everyone's daily mantra to help them secure a positive and productive attitude. *Just let it go.*

3. Complacency

We are all creatures of habit and love living in our comfort zones. I read a quote not long ago that said: "Life begins when you leave the comfort zone." I love it and encourage people to leave their zones often. Comfort is good, but when you're too comfortable you take things for granted and to a certain extent are lazy. Neither is good, and worse yet, you might acquire a sense of entitlement. Working hard and doing things that scare you is your best way to develop an incredible attitude towards work and life. Allow me to share my personal story of leaving my comfort zone.

My Story

I started my career in banking right out of university even though I had majored in sociology and criminology. I did not plan on a career in banking, but like most careers, it was not planned but ventured upon.

I started as a loan administrator, which meant I did a lot of paperwork, filing, faxing and following up on documentation. I soon discovered, as did my manager at the time, that I had a real knack with customers. I was promoted to loans officer, and before I knew it, I became the youngest branch manager, at the ripe age of 23.

My career in the bank spanned almost 20 years, but a phone call on March 27, 1999 changed everything.

By that time, I was quite established in the bank, and given my tenure, the yearly bonuses were substantial. I had a comfortable life with a strong income and I was well respected in the bank. The likelihood of staying there was not unimaginable. I didn't know it then, but looking back, I had always wanted to do more, experience more and more importantly, I knew I was capable of becoming more.

The call was from a colleague who had an opportunity with an international agency. The job called for someone with my training and facilitation background and it meant travel – lots of it – to emerging and developing countries. If it sounds exotic and exciting to you, it was. Incredibly so. But as with many things in life, there was a drawback. The job was on a contract basis, to be renewed yearly.

In today's environment, this does not seem uncommon. In fact, in many organizations it's the norm. However, back then and after a 20-year career with my income, bonus and pension beginning to build up, this was a huge gamble. Welcome to my personal comfort zone! Why should I leave? The money was the same, but the long-term prospects completely unknown.

Luckily for me, I had great family and partner support and so I said good-bye to the bank, and my journey to visit the world began.

My learning curve was steep but worth it. Leaving a tenured position where everyone knows who you are and respects your knowledge, to go in as a virtual unknown is not easy and at times, really not fun. I made mistakes along the way, but with a lot of apologies and lessons learned, I began to thrive in this new role and even learned new languages, and met country presidents and senior government officials. Stretching my comfort zone globally was the best thing I did. I could do this forever!

It's funny how sometimes forever isn't that long. In 2001 my world changed again. My contract, which had been renewed twice already, was about to expire, and given the uncertainty of where international travel was headed, I once again was faced with another opportunity. This time it was to lead a new start-up organization. The autonomy, as well as the ability to share the expertise from my career with the bank and the international organization, was attractive. By that time, I had been on a plane nearly every month and was away for weeks at time. Staying in Toronto felt great.

The new startup was invigorating and was less of a culture shock for me. My comfort zone, however, was still being stretched because if you have ever worked for a startup, you know there are a lot of unknowns and learnings as you go. But I enjoyed it and had the great opportunity to meet with wonderful people and organizations. Life was calmer and more predictable for two years. But then the startup went in a direction that no longer worked for me, and for the first time in my life, an opportunity did not present itself. No one was there to say "Hey, come work for us here!" It was a difficult period in my career because it all seemed like it was for nothing and I'd have to head back to what I knew best – banking. There was nothing wrong with that, but I am a firm believer in moving forward, not backwards. Banking was great to me, but it was in the past and should remain there.

One day, a crazy idea came to me. What if I opened my own training and communications company? Would people hire me to help them? I know, it still sounds kind of crazy to me but I entertained the thought long enough and spoke with enough people who said they would hire me for projects, so I thought "Why not?" The worst that could happen is that I would become a complete failure as an entrepreneur; and banking could always be my fallback. I never burned any bridges and had friends who could help me if I needed help.

My company, Gerry Lewis Inc. (formerly ThinkUp Communications), started in 2004. I had one client. And that client was Scotiabank. They are still my client today and I am fortunate to have been their partner for more than 10 years. In fact, the international agency I worked for after leaving the bank is now a client as well. Ten years later I am here to say that my comfort zone has grown north, south, east and west. But more importantly, with each stretch I never knew if I would be successful, but I was 100% certain that I would do everything possible to make it a success. In fact, writing this book is the result of leaving my comfort zone in 1999. I owe this book to all the people who have helped me see the possibilities and realize things I did not even know back then could be achieved and more.

How did I conquer complacency? I simply took one step across the border of my own comfort zone and then I took another and another and another. I look back now only to see how far I've come, but I also know there are still many more steps to take. I hope I have inspired you to take a few steps yourself.

Life begins the moment you step outside your comfort zone.

4. Conflict

What weighs heaviest on our minds is often unresolved conflict. These are the hurdles of life, and at times these hurdles seem insurmountable, leaving you overwhelmed, angry and not quite sure where to begin. When we live under this dome, our attitudes suffer and nothing seems quite focused. Daily activities, our job, our life feel like we're watching our own movie. We're in it of course, but we're "watching" ourselves and not "being" ourselves.

Mira's Story

Mira works for a bank as a customer service manager. She has more than 20 years at the bank and has been in the same role for most of that time. Mira is someone you would go to before even searching the online manuals or help sites. She can tell you in three easy steps what you need to do to get things done. She is that good. However, in the last 12 months, her team and her manager began to see changes happening. Mira was coming into work agitated and was beginning to snap at her team members. Little things began to get her upset and people started to avoid dealing with her.

When customer service was beginning to be affected, Don, her supervisor, knew he had to speak with her. He asked her out for coffee one afternoon and to his surprise, Mira responded by asking Don if he was going to fire her.

This was the last thing on his mind, but for her to think that really took Don by surprise. Something was clearly wrong.

During coffee Don asked Mira if she had noticed any changes with work that were upsetting her. Anything with her team she wanted to talk about? Perhaps one of the new hires? Mira said work was fine and there was nothing wrong.

Don is a seasoned manager who knows how to probe without being intrusive. He asked about her little boy and how he was enjoying the summer. Mira looked at Don and tears began welling in her eyes. She started speaking but Don could hear only every other word as her sobbing was muffling her words. Don got some tissues and asked Mira to take a breath and share with him what was going on. After a few seconds and a big gulp of her coffee Mira began to talk.

Mira was going through a very tough separation with her husband of 15 years and their son Jacob was right in the middle of it. It didn't help that her family, her biggest support system, lived in the Caribbean and could support her only from afar. Mira was alone and felt she was fighting a daily if not hourly battle with her husband, who had a gambling habit.

He threatened that if she left him, he would do everything he could to keep Jacob away from her. The daily arguments and conflicts made Mira begin to fall apart – and for good reason. She was tackling this alone and feeling as though there was no way out.

How do We Conquer Conflict for Mira?

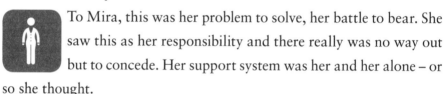 To Mira, this was her problem to solve, her battle to bear. She saw this as her responsibility and there really was no way out but to concede. Her support system was her and her alone – or so she thought.

What Mira (and Don) Did

Something wonderful happens when you share your problem with people who care; they help you take on some of that weight. Don asked Mira if she would let him help her. Don advised Mira that the bank offers services that could be of assistance – if only to talk things through. Mira had known this, but didn't want to make her situation public and feared if others knew, she would have more to contend with. Don assured her of confidentiality and that he would keep this between them.

Don contacted the bank's human resources department and got Mira the support she needed.

But it didn't end there. Don made a weekly appointment with Mira after work to talk through ways Mira could help herself become stronger during this period. At first, Mira just thanked him for his kindness and said there really was nothing he could do. Don corrected her. He told her he was not helping her out of pity, but because he knew her character was that of someone who never let obstacles stand in her way. And yes, this was a big one, but bigger problems mean only that we have more to chip away. "How can we begin to chip this away?" Don asked her.

One of the reasons Mira was feeling down was her constant focus on the problem. She needed to get some space between her and her issue at home, which was consuming her day and night. She needed a distraction – just enough time to be able find some space for herself.

Mira loved going to the gym but had not had time to go for the past year. Don made it a point that Mira extended her lunch hour to go to the gym. At first she thought this was silly and not a good use of her time. But after three yoga classes, she already began to feel stronger and more capable of handling what she had to face at home.

Along with the gym, Don encouraged Mira to start taking smaller steps – mini-goals as Don referred to them. Some of these mini-goals included making sure she had a social outlet with her close friends, who could be her strongest support. Mira also started to take a course in project management offered by the bank. This was an online course and the additional 30 minutes each morning did not affect her routine since she was at work before anyone else. Finally, Mira also started looking at her finances more closely. Being a banker, you tend to take care of everyone else's money but not your own. Not knowing what her future finances would look like, she began taking small steps to ensure she and Jacob had an emergency fund.

With all these small steps, along with the bank's support, Mira suddenly felt less alone, less a one-woman battlefield. She grew stronger as the months passed.

What seems insurmountable and "your" battle alone is not always the case. In fact, when you share your problems with others who care about you, they stand by you and if nothing else, they strengthen you and make you feel less alone. Taking small steps is not silly; in fact it's what can lead to the biggest changes.

In Mira's case, these small steps made her realize she is stronger and more resilient than she ever thought she could be. Mira, in just a few months, returned to the positive, energetic and happy individual she once was, thanks to support from Don and the bank.

Small changes can lead to big outcomes.

"Friendship multiplies joy and divides sad."

— Henry George Bohn, British publisher

5. Change

The inability to go with the flow of change – or the sense of being overwhelmed with change – can destroy anyone trying to maintain a positive attitude. In my previous chapter on Better Tomorrows, we touched on why people react to change differently. However, regardless of how one reacts to change, the fact is: Too much or too rapid a change will overwhelm anyone, and as a result, this affects our attitudes negatively.

While we may not be able to control when change happens, or its intensity or frequency, we *can* control how we think about change and why change can be positive in our lives even though at the time, we are absolutely sure it is not.

The Great Barrier Reef: A Story of Constant Change

About 15 years ago, I heard a story about the Great Barrier Reef and how the challenge of change is necessary for life and growth. I have never forgotten that story and I often reflect on it when I feel as though change has become a little unbearable or frustrating. It has helped me look at change differently – for the most part – although I must admit there are times I too avoid change, but much less so than before.

The Great Barrier Reef is in a part of the Pacific Ocean called the Coral Sea. Stretching more than 2,000 kilometres along the Queensland coast from the mainland towns of Port Douglas to Bundaberg, it was formed well over 2,000 years ago.

The other side of the Reef doesn't have it so easy. The power of the ocean is unforgiving, making life a struggle for 4,000 species of fish, more than 700 species of coral, and thousands of other kinds of plant and animal life.

However, this constant struggle and the ongoing changes caused by the ocean's unpredictable patterns have not prevented growth on this side – quite the contrary. The competition to survive has brought about many different adaptive behaviours and attributes of the Reef's inhabitants. It is in fact this side of the Reef that is known to be the most beautiful, thriving and alive.

Life without struggles and changes that challenge us is much like the marine life on the calmer side of the Reef. It merely exists.

The true beauty of life, of living to the fullest, comes with its daily challenges, struggles and seemingly constant change. Without challenge, life is sedate and its potential is never reached.

In my experience, I have never found my potential until someone said I couldn't do something. I want to thank all the people who told me I "can't." Because of you, I can and I did.

"The secret of change is to focus all your energy not on fighting the old, but on building the new."

– Socrates, Greek philosopher

A Final Word on Attitudes

Your attitude, or how you see the world from the inside, plays a major role in your happiness, success and overall enjoyment of life. Changing your attitude isn't easy and at times you may not even think it's your attitude that needs changing, but someone else's. I encourage you to take a hard look at yours. You may not be able to change someone else's attitude, but you have complete control over yours.

Gerry's Tip

The true beauty of life, of living to the fullest, comes from its daily challenges, struggles and seemingly constant change.

Next time you're feeling generally low and your outlook is less positive than you'd like, ask yourself this question: If I were to think about one of these five parts of my life right now: my confidence, my concerns, my complacency, my conflicts and my changes – is there something that is not where it should be? Is there something I need to pay attention to?

This self-assessment doesn't take long and if you're honest with yourself, it will be one of the best "feel good" tools you can use. It's free; no telemarketer will call you or email you. Even better, this can be done in the privacy of your own thoughts and on the way to work.

Recap

Five culprits of negative attitudes

1. Confidence crushers

2. Concern

3. Complacency

4. Conflict

5. Change

Words to live by

"Let it go."

"Friendship multiplies joy and divides sad."

— Henry George Bohn

"The secret of change is to focus all your energy not on fighting the old, but on building the new."

— Socrates

Ask Gerry

Q I understand that personal attitude is key to achieving success, but all my life I've always worried and thought of reasons why I can't do something. How do I get rid of negative influences in my life and train my mind to be more positive?

A Positive energy begets positive energy. I keep things around me in my office and in my briefcase that make me feel good about myself. And yes, I still have my lucky charm with me. All these things – positive quotes, memorable pictures or images, touchstones – contribute to the way we feel about ourselves. Use them and don't feel they are insignificant. In fact, sometimes, that is all we have to help us get through the day!

Q I never thought of myself as lacking self-confidence, but I do find myself out of place in many social situations. What things can I do in everyday life to gain more self-confidence?

A Finding yourself "out of place" means you are growing and that's always good, even though it's uncomfortable and may seem like the most awkward place to be. I remember my very first conference in university. I was going only as an attendee but I was so nervous about what to expect, what others expected of me, who I would meet, who I would talk to, what if no one talked to me – all the worries anyone would have about a social setting. As I was waiting for the bus to take me to the event, someone came up and asked if I could break their two-dollar bill (yes, we used to have these!) for two ones for the bus. I did not, but I did have an extra token on me so I just gave it to him. He was surprised and very thankful. On his way off the bus he looked at me and said: "Thanks again and take it easy." He didn't know what was going through my mind but the last three words hit me like a bus (no pun intended). "Take it easy." That's exactly what I needed to hear and do. So, I "took it easy" and enjoyed what I still remember as the best conference of my life as a university student.

Q I know I need to work on my attitude, and try to be more positive and confident. What do you think of the concept of "Fake it until you make it?"

A The term "fake it until you make it" doesn't provide the image of who we want to become – an authentic and genuine presenter. However, I would change the perspective on this slightly. Faking it is not about faking to your audience, but to fake it to yourself – more specifically, your brain. Train your brain to think differently about something and it will. Sometimes we are our own worst enemy when it comes to confidence and trusting ourselves and our abilities. Talking yourself up so you believe you are completely capable and are great at something is what I mean when I say "train your brain."

"Believe and you will achieve" is my version of "Fake it until you make it."

✓ My Action Steps to Brighter Thoughts

The next time I'm networking:

The next time I start having a pessimistic thought I will:

_____ (Page 163)

The next time I feel a negative attitude I will conquer it by:

_____ (Page 167)

One immediate step to increase my confidence is:

_____ (Page 170)

My Notes:

Conclusion:
Your Time to Shine

When you shine, and I know you will, you will inspire others. People will look to you for guidance, direction and advice. They will see you as someone who can make things happen, provide peace of mind and, most importantly, as someone who can lead.

When you inspire others, not only will you stand out, get noticed and be seen as brilliant in their eyes, but you will also have an aura about you. You will be stronger, more confident and happier.

There is no secret potion for success and that's a good thing. I have always believed anything worthy of success means you have to work for it, and in the case of communication, you have to work *at* it. Communication, as I've said in this book, is my passion and my purpose. When I know I am able to understand as well as to be understood, I am at my very best and at my happiest.

I hope you have enjoyed this book and will revisit it frequently – like reconnecting with an old friend for some words or ideas you may have forgotten. Even as I was writing this book, I was reminded of so many experiences that helped my career shine.

Sanding out the rough patches of our skills is what makes us better at what we do and who we are as communicators. Just like there is no secret potion for success, there is no overnight transformation. Every meeting, every conference call and every presentation – in fact, every change and every new connection – is your opportunity to improve, refine and perfect. Like an artist looking at his work, look for what you can do to improve the "next opportunity." You are your own individual masterpiece and don't let anyone – and I mean anyone – ever make you feel any less than that.

When we stumble, and we will, it may seem – for that moment – impossible to recover. But know that you will recover and rise above it all. And the sooner you can look at that experience from an honest, courageous and "what can I learn" point of view, you will no longer say *"why me?"* Instead, you will say *"try me"* because you know the next time, you will be better. The next time, you will shine brighter.

I hope you've enjoyed this book and feel stronger as a result. Know that how you communicate and present yourself to others can and does make a difference in your work as well as in other areas of your life.

Always do your personal best, as my mother has said many times. Be relentless in your pursuit of becoming a better communicator. Make this your passion as well and it will be your key to success.

Thank you for reading my book. I hope you will share what you have learned with others and help them when you see they need a helping hand or a comforting word of encouragement. We all need this at some point in our lives.

Some Closing Insights from Mom...

You may notice I have referenced my mother on a number of occasions in the book. And that is for good reason. She is and will always be my inspiration. She is the beacon I can always count on to guide me when life has given me too many balls to juggle and too many distractions to think clearly. Her lessons are timeless and apply to both life and work. I hope you find these useful; they have been invaluable to me.

Give, even though you may not have much to spare. (And she wasn't referring to money.)

Do things for others with no expectations of reciprocity, but just out of the pleasure of giving.

Always give your personal best, in everything you do.

Do not succumb to pettiness and wish for better or more. What you have is exactly what you need, and that is enough.

Have faith in something, anything, and know you have a responsibility to help others and in doing so, you help yourself.

Always do the "right thing" in your heart, even though your mind may be telling you otherwise.

Believe you have everything you need to be successful in life, but never believe you are better than someone else.

And finally: Just be you because you are exactly who you should be!

— *Winnie Lewis (My Mom)*

I shine because of my parents. And in the spirit of these lessons, I wish for you a bright career, one where people will take notice of your brilliance.

It's now your time to shine!

Index

My Notes:

My Notes:

My Notes: